THE DISAPPEARANCE OF LICORICE MCKECHNIE

First edition. July 14, 2021.

Copyright © 2021 Ruth Kanton.

ISBN: 979-8215761694

Written by Ruth Kanton.

THE DISAPPEARANCE OF LICORICE MCKECHNIE

RUTH KANTON

Christina "Licorice" McKechnie

Christina "Licorice" McKechnie was born on October 2, 1945, in Edinburgh, Scotland. She was poetically gifted, and by the time she reached her teenage years, she had written a couple of poems that she absolutely loved, and was willing to share on stage. She started going to folk clubs around Edinburgh, and soon became a frequent figure on the stage. She recited her poems on stage, and would hang out with the other regulars afterwards. One of the people she got acquainted with was Herbert Jansch, who grew up in the residential area of West Pilton in Edinburgh. Jansch was an aspiring musician, and had quit his job as a nurseryman in August 1960 to become a full time musician. He started fulfilling the caretaker roles at the Howff, and with no place to live, usually slept in the local folk club. Without a guitar, he couldn't really choose who to play with, but managed to supplement his income as a novice performer. Sometime in 1961, Jansch was able to find a place to live, and moved in with Robin Williamson. Sometime within the year, Jansch met Licorice and the two hit it off. They spent a bit of time together, and they soon began dating. Licorice and Jansch began having talks about getting married. Jansch was making a bit of money playing in the local folk clubs, and Licorice was performing her poems whenever she had the time. The two were itching to leave Edinburg, and together with Williamson, began exploring their available options. Williamson was also a full-time musician, performing with the local jazz bands. He was looking to shift to a new sound, having fallen in love with traditional music. Williamson and Jansch were looking to move to London, hoping to elevate their music careers to the next level. On her part, Licorice was not really making any solid plans, and was happy to follow Jansch.

For two years, Jansch played in the local folk clubs, and finally felt that he was ready to explore the bigger London scene. He drew his influence from American folk artists like Woody Guthrie and Pete Seeger, and his sound became more in line with the folk sounds. In

1963, Jansch and Williamson finally decided to make their way to the London scene. They were keen on joining the metropolitan folk circuit. Eager to start her new life with Jansch, Licorice left Edinburg with him, the plan being that they would soon get married. When they got to London, their plans seemed to take a much more unexpected path. Jansch and Licorice's wedding plans seemed to progress as planned, and the two even got their marriage banns printed out. Before the wedding, however, Jansch left for Morocco, leaving Licorice and Williamson behind. The relationship was seemingly over.

The Incredible String Band

After Jansch left, Licorice and Williamson became quite close. Williamson and Licorice headed back to Edinburg, and Williamson began playing with Clive Palmer as a traditional folk duo. They played at a weekly club which was run by Archie Fischer at the Crown Bar. By this time, Williamson and Licorice had begun dating, and were living together. Williamson and Palmer began featuring Jansch in some of their performances. However, Jansch set off again, and this time planned to hitchhike throughout Europe. Up until 1965, Williamson and Palmer mainly played in the local folk clubs, with Licorice fading into the background as Williamson's girlfriend. In August 1965, Williamson and Palmer were approached by a talent scout from Elektra Records, Joe Boyd. Interested in what Boyd had to offer, the duo decided to find a third member to fill out their sound. They decided to find someone who plays the rhythm guitar. They held auditions, and ended up choosing Mike Heron, a local rock musician. The trio chose the name "The Incredible String Band."

Palmer began running an all-night folk club in Glasgow, and The Incredible String Band became the house band. Williamson and Licorice began spending a lot of time in Glasgow as Williamson practiced most of his sets at the club. When Boyd became head of the London Elektra office, he once again reached out to the band and asked if they could record an album with his studio. This means that the three would have to relocate to London to create their first album. Once again, Licorice packed up and followed her boyfriend to London. The trio began recording at the Sound Techniques studio in London, with the songs a mix of solo, duo, and trio performances. The album, recorded in May 1966, was self-written, and the three were featured playing a variety of instruments. It is unclear whether Licorice, who had written a number of poems at the time, had helped Williamson on the band's first album. The self-titled album went on to win Melody Maker's "Folk Album of the Year."

After the release of the album, the three went their separate ways. Williamson, together with Licorice, left London and headed to Morocco. When asked when they were planning to come back, Williamson stated that they would stay in Morocco indefinitely. They packed up and left, and many of their friends did not expect them to come back home within the year. However, Williamson quickly ran out of cash, and together with Licorice, found their way back home. Williamson had with him a bunch of Moroccan musical instruments. During Williamson's absence, Heron had gone back to Edinburg and joined a band called Rock Bottom and the Deadbeats. He quickly ditched them when Williamson showed up in Edinburg. The two decided to revive The Incredible String Band.

Williamson and Heron began their UK tour in November 1966, and were supporting Tom Paxton and Judy Collins. On the 4th, they played in the Albert Hall, in London. They played their set in the Free Trade Hall in Manchester on 5th. On 8th, they were in Belfast, playing at the Ulster Hall. On 12th they had made their way to Birmingham, where they played a set in the town hall. The duo had different sounds, and they never attempted to try and collaborate to fuse the sounds. The result was a dynamic set, and they had their music credited to the individual writer. By early 1967, The Incredible String Band was back in London, and Licorice once again packed up and followed

Williamson back to the city. Joe Boyd was once again in the picture, but this time he became the band's manager and producer. The band became a frequent sight in London's folk clubs, playing regularly in a number of London clubs. Boyd, the ever hardworking manager, also secured them a spot in the Newport Folk Festival, which had been started in 1959 by George Wein. The band set off to Newport, Rhode Island, where they joined Leonard Cohen and Joni Mitchell.

In addition to their performances, Williamson and Heron were also working on their second album. The two spent time writing their own lyrics, and would show up at the studio to record one or the other's material. They were credited separately, and never seemed to be interested in coming together to create something that was a bit more collaborative. Boyd described this oddity, "Mike and Robin were Clive's friends rather than each other's. Without him as a buffer, they developed a robust dislike for one another. Fortunately, the quality and quantity of their songwriting was roughly equal. Neither would agree to the inclusion of a new song by the other unless he could impose himself on it by arranging the instruments and working out all the harmonies."

During the recording of the second album, Williamson asked Licorice if she could be a part of the album. He was not offering her a spot on the band, but Licorice was happy to help. She was quickly becoming a more visible figure within the band, and was more than ready to leave the shadow of being just Williamson's girlfriend.

The 5000 Spirits or the Layers of the Onion

Williamson and Heron were looking to shift from the earlier traditional folk sound that The Incredible String Band was known for. While Williamson and Licorice were in Morocco, Heron began experimenting with another instrument, the sitar. Williamson, on his part, came back with a number of exotic instruments that were of African and Middle Eastern origin. They began performances with their new material in early 1967, taking turns playing the instruments while they recorded using a single microphone. Their style began evolving, and the Balmore rehearsals were made of extensive discussions about the arrangement of the instruments. By the time they got into the studio, the duo had already crudely recorded a couple of songs that they wanted featured in the new album. Williamson drew his inspiration from the travels he took with Licorice, and Heron mostly featured his experimental sounds with the sitar. The band began recording at the Sound Techniques studio in Chelsea, with Boyd at the helm. During the various recording sessions, they did employ session musicians to handle the various instruments. It was at this time that Williamson invited Licorice to help the band out.

Unlike their first album, this one featured a new psychedelic sound, with the lyrics touching on a number of themes, including life, mythology, and religion. The album was finally released in July 1967 to raving reviews. The album was well received, peaking at number one on the UK Folk Chart, and number twenty five on the UK Albums Chart. Licorice was on the vocals of the track "Painting Box." While the track was not well received in the UK, it showcased the band's extensive instrumental ability. Williamson asked Licorice to join the band as a full-time member. With the album's success, the band began making more appearances in clubs such as Queen Elizabeth Hall, the Speakeasy Club, and the UFO club. Licorice was now fully performing with the band and a backup voice, and she was on percussions.

The Hangman's Beautiful Daughter

Soon after the release of the second album, The Incredible String Band was back in the studio working on their third album. By this time, Licorice was considered to be a full-fledged member of the band, mostly working as the backing voice in many of the songs. Williamson and Heron were in control of the creative side of the band, although their disagreements were quickly becoming evident to most of the people working with them. However, they were able to agree on the direction of the third album, and were still riding the wave of the success of the second album. With Boyd at the helm, the band was back at the Sound Techniques studios looking to create a masterpiece. The recordings were aimed at creating a sound that would be as close as possible to a live performance. Williamson was still in love with the psychedelic theme, and one of the songs, "The Minotaur's Song," was vividly dreamlike.

Just like the second album, the band's music featured themes of life, esotericism, mythology, and religion. The Minotaur's song, particularly, was a music-hall parody sung from the mythical beast's point of view. Heron wrote "A Very Cellular Song," which featured a number of themes including love, life, and amoebas. Of the ten songs featured on the album, Heron wrote three, while the rest were written by Williamson. The band, still focused on the use of a number of different instruments, saw the members taking on a number of session musicians. Williamson played a great deal of instruments, including the guitar, gimbri, penny whistle, pan pipe, percussion, oud, piano, chahanai, jaw harp, mandolin, harmonica, and water harp. He, together with Heron, did the vocals on the tracks. Heron played the Hammond organ, sitar, hammer dulcimer, guitar, and harpsichord. David Snell was on the harp, while Dolly Collins played the piano and flute organ. Richard Thompson and Judy Dyble were included in "The Minotaur's Song" vocals, and Licorice played the finger cymbals, and was the backing vocals on most of the songs on the album. The album was released in March 1968, and was well received, peaking at number 5 on the UK albums chart. The band was not able to break from the underground scene in the U.S., but the album did reach number 161 on the Billboard Top LP's chart. This album was the most experimental done by the band, and the number of instruments incorporated was hailed by many. Robert Dimery's book, *1001 Albums You Must Hear Before You Die*, featured an introduction by Max Reinhardt, who described The Hangman's Beautiful Daughter as "a potent seed of the current 'world music' movement." He added: "[The Hangman's

Beautiful Daughter] revealed a sustained grandeur of vision, lyrics, and musicality that the group were never to approach again ... Each track is closer to a suite than a song, as Celtic folk, rock 'n' roll, gospel, plainsong harmonies, near qwaali moments, and North African and Indian sonics all drift effortlessly before the ears."

The album, despite a less successful performance in the United States, was nominated for a Grammy. The newfound success saw the band's demand increasing in the country, and they began filling a number of major venues in the U.K. With Licorice in the band, Heron also asked his girlfriend, Rose Simpson, to join the band. As 1968 drew to an end, the band finally went on its nationwide tour, performing in various places including, prestigious rock festivals, open-air festivals, Royal Albert Hall, and Royal Festival Hall. One performance at Fillmore East in New York started a chain of events that no one could have predicted.

Introduction to Scientology

Boyd was content with being in charge of the fast rising band, happy that they had sold out the Royal Albert Hall on numerous occasions, as well as Fillmore West and the Lincoln Center. Boyd was quickly able to secure more and more performances for the band, now composed of Williamson, Heron, Licorice, and Simpson. He met Williamson and Heron in 1965, and he described them as individuals who "had long served as advance scouts into the territories of drugs, Orientalism and mysticism, but they were far from mindless flower children." This was why Boyd had a hard time reconciling what he knew about the band and what happened next. After the band's performance at Fillmore East in New York, Boyd took them to dinner. He recalled that night, "One evening in the autumn of 1968, following a sell-out concert in New York, I took the band to a vegetarian restaurant on East 5th Street, off Second Avenue. To my amazement, the manager of the restaurant was David Simons. He found us a good corner table, where he and I reminisced about long-lost acquaintances from the Cambridge underground."

David Simons was a former dope dealer and harmonica player who Boyd had known in the early sixties. Boyd had assumed that Simons had disappeared into the drug scene, mostly because he'd known him as a "...mumbling, stoned, shambolic figure, witty and sardonic, but seemingly determined to jettison any positive course open to him - in music, for example - in favor of a darker and more chaotic path." He was delighted to see that Simons had transformed into an energetic restaurant manager. Boyd left the band at the restaurant and headed to California for a short business meeting. The next morning, he was called by the band's U.S. manager, who asked for his approval to give the band the cash they made from the mini-tour they were just completing. This deviated so far from how the band's finances were handled that Boyd decided to reach out to the band to find out what was going on. When he called the hotel where the band was staying, he couldn't find them, so he kept trying. Finally, he was able to find Licorice, who gave him a little insight into what had transpired after he left New York.

Licorice told Boyd that the band wanted to pay for some Scientology courses at the Scientology headquarters. Boyd asked them to wait until he got back to New York so that they could have a meeting. Turns out, Simons had joined the band at their table after Boyd left. When they asked him about his transformation, he told them that Scientology saved his life, and went on to invite them to the Church of Scientology New York celebrity center. By the time they left the center later that night, Licorice and Williamson were essentially "converts." Boyd was concerned about the church, especially because most of the things he'd heard about Scientology were not positive. Sensing his reservations, the band decided to wait until they got back to London before making a decision. Boyd was shocked when just a few days after the band got to London, they had already made a unanimous decision. With nothing more to discuss, he gave the band all the cash they were owed. The foursome quickly started the Scientology "auditing" process, which cost about $30 per hour. During the entire time, Boyd was hearing the words "going clear" more and more often, and after some time, he couldn't stand hearing about it. While he was worried about the band, it wouldn't take long for him to start seeing changes.

He said, "I began to notice positive changes in their personalities. All of them had always avoided any discussion of money; now, though, they eagerly convened meetings about the group's finances. It had always been hard to get answers from them about future touring schedules and recording plans; now, such matters were sorted out quickly and efficiently. They even took the time to thank me for the job I was doing for them -previously unheard of. And among themselves, their simmering quarrels and jealousies seemed to evaporate overnight. They stopped taking drugs or alcohol. They became charming company. They never tried to push me into joining."

According to Boyd, "The band had always been fractious - Robin and Mike had no great fondness for each other, while the girls had a barely-concealed mutual contempt," and so the new change looked promising for the band. They began recording new material, and with the new collaborative efficiency that was once lacking, the band quickly released "Wee Tam and the Big Huge," with Licorice playing the percussion, Irish harp, and offering backup vocals. This double LP was released to critical and commercial enthusiasm.

Woodstock Festival and Decline

On May 28, 1969, Michael Lang, the producer of Woodstock Festival, called up the band and offered them $4,500 to perform at the festival. They flew into the festival on August 15, and were scheduled for the 10:30 p.m. slot. The 15th, a Friday, featured many folk-oriented and acoustic acts. However, by the time their slotted time drew close, a torrential rain had started, and the band was worried about getting electrocuted because the stage did not have an overhead cover. Most of the band's instruments were electric, and the risks seemed too much. When Boyd suggested that they play acoustically, the band refused, opting to wait until the rain stopped. In the end, their slot was taken by Melanie, and the band was scheduled to play the next day. At 6:30 p.m. on Saturday 16, Williamson, Heron, Licorice, and Simpson stepped onto the stage to perform after the rock band Canned Heat. A beGlad Winter 1994 article described the band, "Robin's vocals are strong and clear and Likky (Licorice) adds excellent backing vocals while Rose grins and plucks bass and Mike delivers trademark piano. Sartorially, Rose has some sort of diaphanous garb draped about her person. Mike sticks to a simple T shirt and trouser arrangement, Robin in seriously striped trousers and attempted mustache looks very 1969 and Likky deports herself wonderfully in dress and ring of flowers head accessory." Despite their performance, the band wasn't well received in the festival, mostly because Saturday featured mainly rock acts, and their sound was far too different.

In November 1969, the band released their fifth album, Changing Horses. In this album, Licorice and Simpson were fully credited members of the band, and appeared on the cover of the album. Boyd produced the album once more, but by this time, he had noticed a change in the band's creative output. With less disagreements and creative differences, it became clear that they had lost their inventiveness. The album was not a commercial success, with many criticizing its lack of the initial range and creativity that was present in the past two albums. In April 1970, they released another album, I Looked Up. This was also a disappointment to audiences, although some agreed that it was an improvement compared to Changing Horses. The band, by this time, was open about their abstinence from drugs and conversion to Scientology. In 1970, Licorice and Williamson had broken up, and so had Simpson and Heron. Williamson began putting together a show called U, which was described as "a surreal parable in dance and song." The show featured ten dancers and musicians, as well as sets and costumes. Boyd was skeptical about the show, and had a hard time getting promoters on board. But the band, riding the wave of its former successes, decided to go ahead with the show. After a few performances at Fillmore East, the tour was cancelled. Boyd called it a "disaster," and soon sold his production company and stopped managing the band.

By 1971, amidst the band's diminishing success, Simpson left. Licorice did not last long, and left the band in 1972 after they released the album Earthspan.

1972 – 1990

After she left The Incredible String Band, Licorice's life became even more shrouded in mystery. From 1972, Licorice's whereabouts were mostly unknown. In 1974, she was back in the spotlight, this time performing at a Scientology benefit concert which was held in East Grinstead. On stage with her were a number of musicians including Woody Woodmansey, Mike Garson, and Leonard Halliwell. This appearance made it clear that Licorice was still a member of the Church of Scientology, especially since many had begun claiming that she had not converted together with the other members of The Incredible String Band. Sometime in 1976 or 1977, Licorice decided to leave the United Kingdom and moved to California, where she joined the Silver Moon Band. She also worked as a waitress and coatroom attendant, and also performed in bars sometimes. She began dating Brian Lambert, and the two got married soon after. Lambert was a member of Williamson's band. Lambert and Licorice contributed to Williamson's 1977 first Merry Band album Journey Edge, in which she was credited as "Likky Lambert." She then joined Woody Woodmansey's band, U-Boat, but her contribution to the band was never credited or recorded. The band was also short-lived, having one of its last performances at the Reading Festival in 1977.

In the 1980s, Licorice's marriage to Lambert fell apart, and the two went their separate ways, still maintaining their friendship. In 1986, Licorice traveled to Edinburgh to visit her family. It was rumored that she left Los Angeles in 1987, and for two years, lived in Arizona before moving to Sacramento where she allegedly lived for another two years. Many claimed that Licorice was suffering from depression, and that she was behaving in a strange manner during the last times anyone saw her. No one has ever heard from Licorice since 1990, the last time her sister Frances received a letter from her. Frances stated that she was sure that it had been from Sacramento, and that it revealed that Licorice had been recovering from a surgery, but no details were provided.

However, in 2000, an article in Mojo magazine written by Mark Ellen stated that Licorice was "last seen in 1987 hitchhiking across the Arizona Desert. Not even her family has heard from her since." Rose Simpson, Licorice's former band mate, maintained that "There's a possibility she may be dead."

Sightings and Amateur Investigations

Over the years, many have taken it upon themselves to solve the mystery of Licorice's disappearance. Many inquiries have led to dead ends, with many believing that Licorice is still alive and well in California. Rumors circulated that Licorice may have become deeply involved with Scientology, but Heron and Williamson maintained that she quickly became disillusioned with the church's teachings, and may have left. Searches on the Scientology website have not revealed any connection to Licorice.

One amateur investigator looking into her disappearance posted on a forum, stating that Licorice was "alive... and hiding in plain sight [in California]. As far as I can tell, she doesn't really want to be found, so I'm not going to give away anything about her whereabouts on a public forum, but I'm pretty confident that I've located her. Unless I'm quite mistaken, she's still living in California, and quite content with her obscurity. Hopefully she will find her way here one day."

These claims have yet to be substantiated.

Licorice is listed on the LAPD Missing Persons list, although this information is not present on the department's website.

BLACK WIDOW : The True Story of DENA THOMPSON

BRIANNA WELLS

Dena Thompson is a woman who held power over every man that had the misfortune of falling for her charms.

Dubbed a psychopath, Dena succeeded in fooling everyone around her, including investigators, with her lies and charm for over twenty years. Dena would post to Lonely Hearts columns and lure a steady stream of lovers and husbands into her world, eventually leaving each one emotionally and financially bankrupt.

Her first husband lost everything to her and wound up as a desperate man on the run from a mafia threat that did not exist. With one husband gone and his money spent, Thompson would go on to bigamously marry Julian Webb, a successful advertising salesman. In three short years, Mr. Webb would be found dead in his bed from an unexplainable drug overdose. Thompson's third and final husband would soon be fighting for his life when she suddenly attacked him with a bat. Still, somehow, this master manipulator would convince an entire jury that she was nothing less than the victim of abuse. No matter how many fruitless chases she sent investigators on, Thompson would not be able to keep the family members and friends of her victims from stringing the pieces together one at a time.

Her crimes were finally brought into the light of day and she would be imprisoned for her killings.

EARLY LIFE

Dena Thompson was born Dena Holmes in 1960 to a lower middle class family from Hendon, London. Her parents were named Michael and Margaret Holmes. Her father had previously worked as a prison officer but had since retired, and her mother lived as a housewife. Her childhood and teenage years held no indication of unhappiness or abuse and she graduated from school with the highest marks. Her life moved by uneventfully until, at the age of 22, she began a career with the Woolwich building society and met Lee Wyatt on a blind date set up by his cousin, Bob Reed, in 1982. On October 12th the following year, the two married in a registry office and moved into a house just below the South Downs. A small village, Dena and Lee's neighbors describe the quaint area as a "very friendly, happy place to live."

Jackie Howells, a neighbor, described the two, saying: "They were ok. You know, just ordinary neighbors when they first moved here."

Pete Howells, Jackie's husband, recalled that Mr. Wyatt was a relatively private man. "Lee kept himself to himself. You know, [polite] enough to say good morning, um, the usual things, but he was never there long enough to build up a conversation with."

Five years later, in 1987, the seemingly happy couple brought a son into the world named Darren.

Lee was an avid toy enthusiast and established the Denalee Crafts company, combining both of their names. The company would distribute hard and soft toys successfully for a time.

For extra income, Dena continued her second job working for the Woolwich building society in Arundel. Taking inspiration from the success of popular cartoon characters and the money behind merchandising, Lee worked to make his fortune by developing a soft toy character for use in cartoon films.

Their shared endeavor would prove not to be the life changing decision they thought it to be, however, when the firm went belly up and Lee was forced to allow his father-in-law to set him up with a new job at the Bedford Hotel in Brighton. Little did Lee know, that this business failure would flip a previously unseen switch in Dena's heart, hurtling her down a dark path of sex, fraud, bigamy, and murder.

Realizing that her seemingly imminent riches were gone before they began, Dena got her first taste of fraud when she began helping herself to the first installments of 26,000 pounds from the Woolwich building society. At the same time, she began to cast her eyes outward for a new man that could bring her success where she felt her current husband had failed. She soon met and began a passionate affair with Julian Webb, whom she met when he visited her office to sell advertising for the West Sussex Gazette.

Julian put forward the idea of doing a makeover using make up and clothing from local businesses in order to bring in customers. At Julian's suggestion, Dena became the model for this idea, and she was very much in love with the new work.

Julian was an active man, an avid bodybuilder and fisherman until he began a relationship with Dena. Soon, his only hobby was to please his new woman.

Peter Howells describes the moment he first saw Dena with Julian , saying: "One day, looking out the back door, [I] just happened to see Dena and another man kissing on the back doorstep, which was rather strange to say the least."

Dena loved the adrenaline rush of both stealing money and cheating on her husband. It was like a drug for her and attaining this kind of "high" would go on to dominate every action she took for the rest of her adult life.

OUT WITH THE OLD, IN WITH THE NEW

Rosemary Webb, Julian's mother, knew very little about Dena when she and Julian came to her with the announcement that they wanted to marry. Understandably, Rosemary was "a bit taken aback at the speed of this, as they'd only met last May," and they had announced their intentions in August of the same year. Only a fortnight later, wedding cards could be seen decorating the front windows of Dena's home. Neighbors were more than a little confused, since Dena Wyatt was already married. No one had seen Lee in weeks and it was as if he disappeared off the face of the earth.

Julian and Dena married on December 2nd, 1991, and Julian did not know that the marriage was bigamous.

Without Julian's knowledge, Dena had sent her first husband running for the hills only months before their marriage. Dena and Lee had signed up for the mortgage on their home together in Yapton, West Sussex. Three months later, in the year of 1991, Denawould give her husband stunning news. She claimed the two needed to separate because Lee was about to come into a large fortune, as there was allegedly a multi-million dollar deal being set up with Walt Disney over his stuffed toy named "Shaun the Leprechaun."

She told him that the mafia was now out to kill him for a cut of the money.

In order to make the lie more believable to Lee, as well as their friends and family, Dena forged letterheads from well-known toy company in the U.S. and showed them to her husband, writing up a lucrative contract that only required his signature.

Lee fell so completely for the deception that he quit his job at the Bedford Hotel.

On June 30th, a debt collector appeared at the door. Dena told her husband to run for his life while she intercepted the man. Lee would run out the back door, praying he would get away unscathed.

Fearing for his family's well-being, Lee Wyatt went on the lamb, but Dena would not allow him to fully disappear without also convincing him to write a series of letters framing himself for the Woolwich building society fraud as she continued to steal more and more money through false accounts.

In an interview taken years later, Lee was quoted saying: "She lives a life of lies and fantasy, and I was the mug who went along with it."

Lee Wyatt gave himself a new name after going on the lamb, Collin Mitchel, and sought work in the Cornish seaside resort of Newquay. The man that eventually gave him work, David Rodd, was the manager of Carousel Amusements. He stated that Lee came in "to get away from his life in West Sussex, which was nothing strange at the time because a lot of people work for the summer, or something like that." Employees described the mysterious man as easy going and easy to talk to, happy to go out with coworkers for drinks. The job even came with a flat above the establishment that Lee rented for a place to stay. When coworkers eventually learned of his true identity much later, they were more than a little shocked.

A coworker, Mark Pope, laughed about the absurdity of such a sudden revelation, stating in an interview: "Maybe that's why when we were shouting 'Collin' he wasn't replying. We thought he might have been a little bit deaf."

For three years, Lee hid from the invisible boogeymen his cheating wife had created.

Dena, on the other end, set up shop with Julian in the house that Lee had purchased.

Lee sent most of the money he earned to his wife while he lived as a vagrant, believing that any moment his wife would call him, let him know the danger had passed, and finally tell him he could return home to the loving wife and son that awaited him. Dena, however, held no intentions of allowing him to do so, using the money he sent to fund her second wedding and even going so far as to create a gang of fictional assassins called "The G-Men" that were constantly on the hunt for their prey.

Each time Lee called home, praying that at last the "hunt" had been called off, Dena would insist he stay hidden.

Her current beau, Julian, would not be her only suitor during this time as neighbors would recount other men coming in and out of the home while her husband was away at work. There were even a few close calls in which a visitor would be leaving the home almost at the same time as Julian pulled in for lunch, something he did daily.

Christopher Cordess, a legal adviser on Dena Webb's case, had this to say of her: "She has an enormous ability to project, but this is an intense form of it. It had a sort of psychotic flavor, that is a crazy flavor, so intense that it makes people by some extraordinary mechanism -which I can't explain- has an influence over people that makes them do things which their normal selves would never do or do again."

LIES, LIES AND MORE LIES

Early on in her marriage with Julian, Dena informed her husband that she was terminally ill, and that her employer was threatening to fire her because she had taken so many days away from work due to her sickness.

Julian saw this as outrageous as Dena would look the part, acting weak and lethargic. In reality, however, Dena was being fired because 26,000 pounds were missing from accounts at the Woolwich building society, and she was being investigated for it. She claimed that her first husband, Lee, had returned and had been threatening her, blaming him for the missing money. Dena alleged that her first husband was sending her threatening letters and even secretly recorded him making threatening phone calls to her.

Dena then claimed to her neighbors, the Howells, that Lee had come to her home and raped her. The police took her false accusations seriously, and Lee Wyatt finally became the wanted man he had always wrongly believed he was.

Furious of his situation, Lee returned home whilto confront Dena while Julian was upstairs sleeping. Dena refused to explain anything and managed to turn him away. Little did she know that her web of lies had already begun to fall apart at the seams and her subsequent downfall was imminent.

In 1994, Dena took the final step in her downward spiral of darkness: murder. Detectives believe at this time Julian may have begun to discover the extent of his wife's lies before she took his life with a massive overdose of dothiepin, an anti-depressant, and aspirin hidden in his curry over the course of some days.

Julian loved curry with extra spice, a fact that Dena took advantage of to mask the bitter taste of the poison.

It was on Julian Webb's birthday, June 30th, that his devious wife first informed Julian's mother over the phone that her son had fallen ill and had in fact been sick since Tuesday, two days before.

Dena told his mother that her son had "stayed in the sun too long" and had drunk himself into a stupor, which struck his mother as strange.

She knew that her son didn't partake in alcohol.

Friends and work colleagues of Julian had their suspicions as well, as it was very unlike him to be so sick and to not check in with his loved ones. After his second day of missed work, a male co-worker called to inquire if Julian was okay.

"Oh, well, he's sick," Dena said before hanging up on the man. A number of people called the house inquiring after Julian's health, and each caller would receive a vague, fantastic story as to why he could not come to the phone or work.

At 1:30 a.m. in the morning, on Julian's birthday, Dena would ring the doorbell at the Howell residence, waking them.

She told them that she could not wake up her husband and that he was not breathing. When Dena finally called for help, her husband was long dead and rigid in his bed.

Dena presented the police with two bottles, alleging that her husband had taken an overdose of antidepressants and aspirin on purpose. This was a hard pill for his family to swallow, however, as Julian was a fitness fanatic. He never drank or even took aspirin as he was regimented toward clean living.

"I was awake when the police came 'round to tell me what had happened," Julian's mother recalled. "And I knew as soon as I saw them, before I'd spoken to them, and I heard the police car from upstairs. I just knew."

Julian Webb died of an overdose on his 31st birthday in his bed, at least two hours before an ambulance was called.

Julian's coworkers recall coming up to their work building and finding Dena sitting on the front steps a very short time after his death. She was described as moving between crying and lucidity, and the way she seemed to go between the two so quickly unnerved those that witnessed it. Dena is reported to have said in the same breath, "Julian's dead. I need to speak to someone about the insurance money." To any sane person, these two sentences could not possibly be said in the same conversation, much less the same breath, and yet here was this woman wearing a nightgown and jacket, saying just that.

Dena told the police that her husband committed suicide, but his apparent good health and happy attitude prior to his "sickness" prompted police to investigate. They would discover that the antidepressants belonged not to Julian Webb, but to Dena. Still, the pills were kept in a drawer in the kitchen, where Julian could have easily found and taken them, and thus the fact the pills belonged to Dena held little weight. Though the coroner could not confirm that he had taken the dose accidentally, there was not enough evidence to prove foul play so the medical examiner recorded an open verdict.

Wasting no time, Dena attempted to collect thirty-five thousand pounds from Julian's pension plan which was to be released in the event of his death. Julian's mother would not allow her son's murderer to get away with his life and his money, however, and she was able to quickly establish that Dena was not his next of kin as she was still legally married to her first husband.

Dena also attempted to have Julian's remains cremated, but his family and investigators were able to successfully prevent such an evidence damaging act. It would not be until her trial for attempting to murder her third husband, however, that Julian's body would be exhumed.

The funeral was held at a church on Hayling Island in Northney. Dena Webb showed up wearing a high-riding mini-skirt and a blouse that revealed her ample cleavage.

The right side of the church was packed with friends and family mourning the loss of their Julian, and to the left sat the lone figure of Dena in sexy attire. Friends and colleagues describe Dena's face as emotionless and noticed that the flowers she brought appeared to have been taken from the cemetery nearby.

Much to his family's dismay, Julian's death was eventually ruled an accidental overdose, and Dena Webb moved on in her hunt for a new man to take deadly advantage of.

The freshly widowed Dena looked for love by advertising in the personal ads, describing herself as a "bubbly blonde."

No one proved clever enough to resist her charm. Businessmen, teachers, a prison officer, and even a convicted rapist fell under her ruthless spell before she dumped them or vanished. Detectives believe Dena successfully conned her victims out of a total of a half-million pounds.

One of her victims, Robert Waite, was found and interviewed. He had worked with Dena in 1980 and, years later, suddenly received a card from her inviting him to a reunion party. He called her, and Dena invited him to dinner then seduced him.

Dena would tell Waite that Julian had died from an overdose of steroids and that her first husband, Lee Wyatt, had beaten and attacked her regularly. Waite believed her, as he had no reason not to. But when Mr. Waite began to pull away out of disinterest, Dena quickly convinced him that she was dying of a terminal illness. Wishing to help a dying woman, he promised to take her to one of her favorite places, Florida, to care for her during her last months of life. After they arrived, while the two were lying in bed at a motel, Waite woke to feel a sharp prick in his side. He became entirely sure that Dena drugged him and slept through an entire day.

Soon after, Dena left him for broke, saying she had to appear as a witness in an anti-mafia trial in New York. She was actually flying back to Britain as she was due to appear in court for defrauding the Woolwich. For three weeks, Waite was stranded. Evenually, he came back to England and on August 31st, 1995 he discovered that Dena Webb had just been convicted of fraud and sent to jail. It was revealed during this trial that Dena had falsified the alleged death threats sent to her by mail from Lee Wyatt, and even his recorded calls were scripted by her. At the time of their creation, Lee believed that he was creating them to protect his family. The police were able to conclude that Lee was in fact hundreds of miles away during the time of the thefts working in Newquay under an assumed identity, and the charges against him were dropped. Dena was released after only nine months, and she soon returned home.

A NEW MAN, ANOTHER SUCKER

Richard Thompson was just another name on the long list of pockets Dena wished to empty when he discovered her personal ad in a Lonely Hearts column. The two met and "hit it off", marrying in a Holiday Inn in Florida.

The two were forced to round up strangers, one of which was the manager of the hotel, as witnesses after Dena's supposed "friends and family" did not show.

Thompson had money and owned a home in an affluent community which Dena found to her liking. She lied and charmed Thompson, claiming a love of deep-sea fishing which was his favorite hobby.

Dena told Richard that she had won the lottery and could access the money in the States, and so the loving couple made plans to travel overseas and claim her winnings. After the trip had been finalized, Dena enthralled her new husband with ideas of becoming

"a big game ocean skipper" and opening a fishing company.

This inspired Richard to attend classes run by the U.S. Coast Guard. He passed his boating exam, a feat that did not come without a huge amount of hard work. Richard then took an early retirement, and his wife used the money to renovate his cottage in order to rent it out while they were away in Florida building their new life. The new Mrs. Dena Thompson then suggested they combine their financial assets, a suggestion that the blissfully in love Richard saw as a reasonable thing to do. He even made out his will to his wife, giving her power of attorney over his financial affairs. Not long after this, Dena allegedly asked him if their waste disposal unit might be powerful enough to crush bones. A chilling question, to be sure, but a question that Richard thought little about.

Unfortunately for Richard, his wife had a murderous surprise in store for him just one day before the couple were to leave for the States.

On that fateful night, according to Richard's testimony, his wife had promised him a wild round of rough, kinky sex which was something he eagerly accepted.

Before getting ready, Dena locked their German Shepard, Oden, away in another room. She then informed her husband that a man would be coming the following day with a green card for him, which he would then be able to use to go to Florida.

She then started to run a hot bath and told him to "get ready for some fun."

With her husband anticipating something kinky, he allowed Dena to tie up his hands and feet.

"Get ready for a night to remember," she cooed, placing a towel over his face.

Dena then picked up a baseball bat and cracked it over his head. Once then twice for good measure.

Stunned with blood pouring into his eyes, Richard jerked and twisted his body enough to loosen the restraints on his wrists. He sat up but Dena was ready for him.

Grabbing a butcher knife from the night stand beside their bed, she stabbed him in the shoulder. Still dazed from the baseball bat hits to the head, Richard miraculously recovered and pushed Dena away.

Dena slipped on his blood on the floor. Richard seized the advantage, pushing his thumb into her eye. Dena went for the knife again but Richard pushed harder with his thumb.

"I'll put your eye through your head if you don't let go of the knife," Richard warned.

THE AFTERMATH

It would be several days after Richard fought for and won his life that the idea to check his bank accounts would suddenly come to him. A quick call had his accountant checking his assets, and sure enough, it was discovered that Dena, the woman he had grown to love, had cleaned out his bank accounts. She also made inquiries about surrendering his 89,000 pound life insurance policy and put up his house for sale without his knowledge.

"I fell for her personality," Richard said afterward. "I trusted her 100 percent."

Dena was put on trial for attempted murder and fraud, with Richard as the key witness.

She would plead not guilty and her attorney claimed it was Richard who attacked his wife, becoming violent when she told him that Florida had all been a lie, and that Dena had hit him with the bat in self-defense.

The jury fell for Dena's charm as well, acquitting her of attempted murder.

The district attorney would call the case his "the most staggering court verdict I ever had."

Dena was, however, sentenced to three years and nine months at Lewes Crown Court on fifteen counts of fraud, involving thousands of pounds that she stole from her husband Richard, as well as two other lovers. Not only had Richard been nearly murdered without warning, but now he was financially bankrupt and emotionally devastated. During the trial, Dena admitted that her husband was not the only one she had defrauded, and she was convicted to eighteen months in jail for stealing 26,000 pounds from her old employer, the Woolwich building society, by setting up fake accounts. She had also stolen 5,000 pounds from a former boyfriend.

"I had never seen such a miscarriage of justice," Richard said. "It was appalling."

Dissatisfied with the outcome of the trial, the police began an investigation into Dena's past and quickly discovered some disturbingly repetitive facts. They discovered a long train of men left destitute in the wake of the "bubbly blonde" that promised them love and companionship. They also took a second look at the fate of her late husband, Julian Webb, and the cruel lies that sent Lee Wyatt into homelessness for three years. Immediately following their discovery of Julian Webb's death and the investigation into Dena regarding his overdose, investigators reopened the case and exhumed Julian Webb's body for further examination. For six years, Dena Thompson had gotten away with murder, but the attack on her current husband would prove to be her undoing.

Forensic scientists confirmed that antidepressants caused his death, but concluded that the medication was administered over a period of time rather than all at once. This ruled out Dena's original claim of suicide and made it clear that Julian had in fact been poisoned over the course of a week. Scientists were able to prove this by examining his stomach and blood content. The last days of Julian Webb's life would have been horrific. Isolated from his friends and family, Julian would lie dying in his bed, knowing something was wrong but unable to help himself or reach out to others. All the while, Dena nursed him, likely feeding him by hand in what must have appeared to be an act of love and devotion. Instead, this monstrous psychopath was dosing him with still more and more antidepressants and aspirin.

Julian's final moments would have been filled with agony as his body shut down, with Dena's emotionless face being the last thing he would ever see.

Nine years after his untimely demise, Julian Webb's killer would finally be brought to justice. In 2003, Dena Thompson received life, with a minimum of sixteen years, for murder.

FINALLY...

Dena Thompson was a master manipulator of people, with one husband murdered, another almost murdered, and a third on the run and penniless.

The Recorder of London, Michael Hyam, is quoted saying to Mrs. Thompson that her crimes were "utterly ruthless and without any pity. Nothing can excuse you for the wickedness of what you did."

Immediately after the conviction, UK investigators put together a large scale search for any and all of Mrs. Thompson's previous victims with the fear that they had a serial killer on their hands. The search took investigators and Interpol across the length of Europe to Bulgaria, where Dena had been a regular visitor throughout the late 1970s and early 1980s. One Bulgarian boyfriend by the name of Stoyan Kostov was never found, and the fear is that he was an early victim of Dena who was no referred to as the "Black Widow." How did she make her way to Bulgaria?

Dena was an avid gymnast at a young age, although she never chose to compete, and her father, Michael Holmes, was highly involved in the sport. This is allegedly how Mrs. Thompson's Bulgarian connections were made.

Inspector Martyn Underhill felt a certain sense of urgency when searching for Mr. Kostov (last known address: 27 K.D. Avramov Street, Svishtov), but was unable to find the man.

"We cannot rule out the possibility that other partners have been injured in some way," Inspector Underhill said.

Dena visited Bulgaria for several years, with her gymnastics connections said to be her reason. Much mystery hangs over these visits and the still missing Kostov, and it is suggested that Dena's murderous ways began long before she ever met Julian Webb. If Kostov is indeed Dena Thompson's first victim, he could be the only person on earth capable of shedding light on what turned Dena towards a life of crime.

The investigation came to an eventual end, however, when no solid evidence could be found on any murders prior to Julian Webb. Some, including a UK journalist named Adrian Gatton, believe that there is much more to the Bulgarian story than could be found by police. It is suggested that the operation carried out by Interpol and West Yorkshire police was done half-heartedly, as they may never have visited Bulgaria.

There are likely many unnamed men made victims by Dena Thompson's grandiose lies, but they might feel too embarrassed to come forward and identify themselves. It is proven that she stole from a dozen different men, but police believe the number to be much larger. Dena Thompson maintains her innocence, and her most recent appeal against conviction has failed.

In 2007, she was sentenced to a minimum of sixteen years in prison.

GOLD DIGGER VIRGINIA LARZELERE

SAMANTHA RUE

Virginia Larzelere: Incarcerated and spared the electric chair

Mid-afternoon shots rang out in the middle of a suburban dental clinic almost 27 years ago. A frantic call was received by emergency dispatch. The call was made by the wife of the slain dentist yelling down the line for assistance to save her husband's life, following a fatal gunshot wound to the chest.

March 8, 1991 was the day that changed Virginia Larzelere's life forever. The cold-blooded murder of her dentist husband Norman Larzelere sparked off a chain of events that culminated in her lifelong incarceration. Although it could be proven that she never pulled the trigger on her husband, the prosecution successfully argued that she was the mastermind behind the crime. Police investigating the crime scene discovered that as Norman lay dying in a pool of blood he mumbled, "Was that Jason?"

Jason was his son, adopted when he had married Jason's mother.

The investigation would result in a bizarre set of confessions that implicated Virginia Larzelere in the murder for money case. Psychiatric and hearsay evidence pointed to the motive of death to be avarice and a psychopathic manipulation of men throughout her life. Although Virginia's death sentence was commuted to life in 2008, she asserts she is still innocent to this day.

The Crime: Murder at midday, March 8, 1991

The masked killer silently entered through the back door of the dentist's surgery, with a sawed-off shotgun held by his side. His mission was to kill Norman Larzelere, possibly for the life insurance money in some sort of deal with Virginia. The sound of footsteps alarmed Norman as he had not heard anyone enter through the door.

During the trial, Dr Larzelere was reported to have said, "Who's there?" The other occupants of the office at the time were his wife

Virginia and the state's witness, Kristen Palmieri who barely looked up when Norman went into the corridor to find out what the disturbance was.

Testimony provided in the first murder hearing alleged that upon seeing a gunman in the shady office corridor, he yelled, "No!" and ran back into the office slamming his office door behind him. The gunman who was in close pursuit was able to pull the trigger once, shattering through the door and hitting the doctor's chest. He subsequently died at the scene from a combination of chest trauma causing a pneumothorax (collapsed lung) and fatal blood loss.

His wife, Virginia, rushed to his side and yelled for someone to call 911. The report from the ambulance dispatcher subsequently reported that Virginia yelled to the 911 dispatcher, "Someone just came in and shot my husband! Somebody shot my husband!"

As Norman's life seeped away, she cradled him, crying. The witness alleged that he asked Virginia, "Where's Jason? Was that Jason?" By the time the police and ambulance had arrived, the gunman had fled, leaving behind a trail of devastation and turmoil. Just as he had sneaked into the clinic without being detected that fateful afternoon, as he was able to leave with none of the witnesses able to positively identify him.

The question, "Was that Jason?" uttered by the dying man, formed the basis of an investigation, where the prosecution's case pinning the murder of Dr Norman Larzelere on Virginia's biological son, Jason.

Betrayal, Lies, Manipulation

Piecing together the various players in this shocking murder for money was the task of Detective Dave Gamell. His first major lead came from the confession of Steve Heidle who had called the detective in May to reveal his hand at disposing of the murder weapon. He claimed that he had been directed by Virginia to clean the weapon in muriatic acid and then bury it in concrete.

Heidle claimed that he was aided in his endeavours by the witness Kristen Palmieri, who like himself, was employed by the slain victim's wife, Virginia Larzelere. Both of them gave statements saying that Virginia had blackmailed them into doing terrible things. Heidle also confessed to knowing about a plan to kill Norman for his life insurance and he alleged that she paid her son Jason $200,000 to kill his adopted father and benefactor.

Heidle, like many others that were unveiled during the investigation, was used as a pawn of Virginia Palmieri to assist in the hiding of evidence. Heidle spent hours with Gamell and provided a lot of useful evidence, not just about disposing the weapons but also about the family dynamics at play that led to the murder being committed by Jason.

According to the state prosecutors, the main motive for killing the well-respected and loved dentist was to bank the payout from Norman's recent increase in life insurance, which had been in place just prior to his untimely death.

Heidle claimed that Virginia had an insatiable appetite for men and money. He also claimed she lived a life filled with drugs and crime all of which made him intimidated to stand up to her. He told Detective Gamell, that if she could get her husband killed in broad daylight, then he feared for his own life if he did not do as instructed. He agreed to hide the evidence and buried the gun deep in the waters of Pellicer Creek.

That same afternoon following Heidle's confession, Kristen Palmieri was called for questioning. She corroborated Heidle's account of the events, telling the detective that she knew that hiding the weapons was wrong. She said that she had never believed that Jason could have been the murderer but subsequently Jason had confessed to her that he had been forced to kill his father at Virginia's behest.

Sure enough, police divers uncovered a plastic container with a rusted shotgun embedded in concrete in Pellicer Creek. In exchange for turning state's witness, Heidle and Palmieri were granted immunity from further prosecution.

Following this significant piece of evidence, Virginia Larzelere was caught and arrested by police the following day. It was said she was attempting to flee from Edgewater with a lot of cash and jewellery in her purse. Detective Gamell had years of experience in homicide investigations and claims he could detect her fake mourning. "I've dealt with a lot of murders and a lot of deaths," Gamell said. "And you know when someone mourns legitimately and when someone's overacting. That's how she seemed."

Gold Digging and Incest: the prosecution's case

As the state's case against Jason and his mother unfolded, it was Heidle's statements to police that provided ample motive for the crime. Heidle claimed that he'd overheard a conversation between Jason and Virginia where she had said that she'd increased the life insurance policy and forged his signature. Dr Larzelere had no suspicions of his wife's dark intentions. Heidle's sworn statement reads, "She said she's [forged] all of Norman's legal documents and it was no big deal." Evidence presented in court revealed that prior to the murder, there had been an increase on the value of the life insurance from $1 million to $2.1 million. Furthermore, a few weeks before the murder, it appeared that his will had been amended to favor his wife. Previously, she was not listed as a sole benefactor.

The trial was a field day for sensationalist journalists who reported on the case. There were many scandalous angles to report. Virginia had already been involved in an embezzlement scheme some years before. Although the charges had been dropped, it was clear that the many people in her life (such as the key witness Heidle) did not like her. It was argued that Virginia was a heartless gold digger who had a long history of manipulating all the men in her life in order to get better resources and status.

While Norman had been dearly loved in Edgewater, it was the belief of many in the small town, that Virginia's arrival in his life was a targeted and calculated move by her. She was a ruthless femme fatale who saw the married dentist as an easy mark. Norman had divorced his wife soon after beginning an affair with Virginia and they married within two months of the divorce being finalized.

Heidle was the key witness and he gave evidence throughout the trial of many instances that implicated Virginia with the murder. Allegations were that Norman Larzelere's life insurance policy and will were forged were denied by Larzelere's defence attorney, Jack Wilkins.

Wilkins was an attorney who loved representing members of the rich party crowd to which Virginia belonged. He claimed that it was great to represent this echelon of drug-taking socialites, as they always paid in cash. Wilkins seemed more like *Breaking Bad's* Saul Goodman, flamboyantly representing drug dealers and winning on minor technicalities.

Wilkins was more a party boy than a lawyer, and while he did have credibility in winning some prominent cases, he lacked the experience to deal with serious forensic evidence. Although he won a prominent civil rights case permitting a small town cinema to sell pornographic movies, he was simply out of his depth in a murder trial.

Virginia's poor choice of lawyer was to seal her fate. Wilkins was a dreadful choice to represent her as he'd admitted, "I'd never done a capital murder case before." During Larzelere's appeal case, evidence was tendered to the court to show that Wilkins had a very serious substance abuse problem, with daily use of vodka, cocaine and methamphetamines. Wilkins did try to turn down the case, but Virginia insisted on retaining him.

The relatively inexperienced and often inebriated Wilkins had to go up against the surgical-like precision of Special Prosecutor Dorothy Sedgwick's argumentative style. Appointed by the District Attorney, Sedgwick was chosen for her assassin-like instincts to win at all costs. She ran a vicious case against Virginia calling into question the background of the accused.

It was only in the subsequent appeal hearings against the death sentence that many important facts about Virginia's early life were brought to light. Much of the blame for this apparent miscarriage of proper judicial process can be laid at Wilkins' feet. Even Sedgwick was on the record commenting that a decent defence lawyer would have called witnesses to refute some of the state's evidence. Wilkins never sought the opinion of a psychiatrist nor any other expert to take the stand on Virginia's behalf.

The multi-generational level of neglect and sexual misconduct towards children was the key to the prosecution case. Court reports show that under psychiatric questioning, it was clear that as a child growing up, Virginia believed that sexual behavior with family members was the norm. This allowed the prosecutor to paint Virginia as a ruthless killer. In other words, if she was a murderer, being an incestuous murderer made it all the more salacious and perhaps believable to the jury who ultimately convicted her of the murder of Dr Norman Larzelere.

Under Sedgwick's direction, the jury was directed to focus on Virginia's apparently insatiable appetite for men and money as the primary motivation for the murder plot. Sedgwick presented psychiatric evidence to prove that Virginia had a personality disorder which caused her pathological love of money and control.

In the trial, Virginia was successfully portrayed as a manipulative woman with psychopathic tendencies who seduced her son Jason to murder his father, in order to benefit from the life insurance claim. She then used money and blackmail to gain the loyalty of people such as Heidle and Palmieri and her own children.

The state was unable to convict Jason and he was acquitted in 1992 as there was insufficient evidence to place him at the scene of the crime that fateful March day in 1991. However Virginia's guilty verdict and death sentence stayed. It was always clear that she did not murder her husband by her own hand, but suspicions remain as to her collusion due to the circumstantial evidence

How did it come to this?

Virginia grew up in the 1950s in a small town called Lake Wales, 60 miles south of Orlando, Florida. She was the oldest of four daughters all living with their Mom and Dad in a three bedroom bungalow in the working class part of the town. Both of her parents worked in a local juice company called Donald Duck.

Dr Mosman, the psychiatrist giving evidence in the appeal case told the court that she had confided to him that her father, "Pee-Wee" Antley, was a strong dictator whose moods ruled the house of women. It was noted he was a huge drinker who sexually abused each of his daughters (and subsequently Virginia's own children Jessica and Jason). In an interview with the Miami New Times in 2013, Virginia said, "sexual abuse doesn't only happen in poor households, does it?"

Virginia's younger sister, Peggy, testified that Virginia took more of the sexual abuse from their father in an attempt to spare her younger sisters. The abuse would gave birth to a burden of silence, of not being able to confide in people outside the family or to get any help for them or their mother. Mosman revealed to the court that the father was, "a chronic alcoholic, sitting on the porch drinking daily, with no outside hobby or social interests."

Virginia left home at the age of seventeen but the scars of abuse never left. Having been a victim of abuse from as young as the age of three, the emotional and sexual trauma stayed with her and influenced her outlook on life and on men. Virginia knew that the best way to survive was to use men to gain access to the wealth that she needed to feel free from her demons.

Her success at attracting many men (she was married three times by the time she was in her early 30s) came about because she was able to use her looks and sexual conduct to acquire goods and status throughout her life. Even Virginia's daughter Jessica (from her first marriage to Harry Mathis), said that the child abuse she had suffered led her to be ruthless and impulsive. Jessica has stated in an interview some years ago that, 'My mother is a very intelligent woman, who had looks which she used to her advantage." The state's case relied on this aspect of her love of the high life and of sexual promiscuity to draw the sketch of her as a ruthless gold-digging murderer.

The entire prosecution case was based on Heidle's voluntary testimony, which painted Virginia as the product of a dysfunctional and incestuous family. It was alleged that her exposure to serious childhood abuse and trauma led to her manipulative and ruthless tendencies. However, no psychiatrist was ever called by the defence to undertake an evaluation of her mental state.

Virginia's teen marriage

In Lake Wales where Virginia was growing up, she did not have any friends. This is because her domineering father felt the need to protect his filthy secret from authorities so visitors were restricted from visiting the home.

Virginia attended and graduated from Lake Wales High school and immediately fled home to marry Harry Mathis when she was only 17 years old. Soon after the marriage, she fell pregnant with Jason and then Jessica. Experts say that people often people who have dysfunctional parents often choose dysfunctional partners, and this certainly appears to be the case with Virginia.

She was trapped as a young mom, from a dysfunctional background now living with an abusive husband. Harry Mathis beat his wife and son Jason, as evidenced in the police records. Virginia divorced him in 1978, determined to be as far away from his abuse as possible, and wanting a new life for her two young children, Jason and Jessica. Instead of seeing her getting away from Harry as a triumph against abuse, the prosecutor used this to demonstrate that Virginia 'burned through' husbands. The prosecutor even used the fact that she wished for her abusive ex-huband's death as evidence of her murderous intent for Norman.

However, despite the various setbacks, abuse and domestic violence there remained in Virginia evidence of a clear determination to not only survive but thrive. Once she had escaped her parental home of horror, she went into another dysfunctional marriage for a brief period. It is also a fact that she had turned to substances to numb the emotional pain from a young lifetime of abuse. She was clearly not the most stable woman in Edgewater, but she was a survivor.

Leaving Mathis started her love of freedom, and of the partying good life that has been portrayed through documentaries about the case.

Socialite in the making

Having been divorced at the age of 25, and with two young children in tow, Virginia was clearly on a mission to find a man that would replace their biological father as a role model in her life. Being denied a good role model of appropriate masculinity, she was easily distracted by the promises of various men simply looking for a woman to bed. However, she was also hungry for money and status but preferred freedom to being tied to a man It appears that her main goal since leaving home at 17 had been to free herself from the control of a man.

Her hunger for a better life, even being married three times before she was 32, demonstrates a decision to turn away from the cycle of abuse that her mother had endured. Virginia's mother stayed by her husband's side through the mistreatment and abuse of all of his daughters. In a sense, her mother colluded with him by permitting the abuse to be perpetuated, child after child. Her misplaced loyalty for, and fear of, her husband kept her at his side.

Virginia's drive to be different from her passive mother showed her adventurous spirit, her impulsiveness and her keen business sense. By the mid-1980's she had worked her way up to being the president of a construction company based in the little town of Edgewater, a seaside town, two hours north of her hometown, Lake Wales. Although Edgewater was still a very small and isolated town, she had successfully changed her fortunes. Her financial success had become like a drug It made her feel good, and the more she did of it, the better she felt.

Her stars changed completely in 1985 due to the happenstance of a dental appointment where she was to meet the love of her life. It was in Dr Norman Larzelere's dental surgery that love was born. Virginia claims that from that first meeting she knew he was 'the one'. The feelings were clearly mutual, as the already married dentist quickly divorced his wife so that he could make a life for Virginia and her children. He embraced Jason and Jessica as his own and officially adopted them when they married.

"There was nothing but love in that household," fhe family's housekeeper Juanita Washington said. "Nothing but love." Upon their marriage, the newlyweds Virginia and Norman promptly moved into a mansion in a prestigious uptown area. The home had previously housed all sorts of people from the higher echelons of society including congressional representatives and bank presidents. By all accounts, despite the differences in their social standings and backgrounds, they seemed to be deliriously happy and to be true soul mates.

Storm clouds over paradise

However, things started to get a bit difficult the following year as Virginia's business went bankrupt amid allegations of embezzlement. Settling out of court, all criminal charges were dismissed. Around this time, her teenage son Jason was getting a bit out of hand, as teenagers in blended families often do.

Jason was a known party boy in the local Orlando gay club scene. He also befriended drag queens and seemed to have inherited his biological father's love of beating women."He threw me down the stairs and broke my ribs by kicking me over and over again," his sister Jessica recalled. "I had told my dad that Mom was cheating on him with a patient of his." Jason staunchly defended his mother and allegations of her sexual appetites together with her son's strong filial devotion was a source of gossip surrounding their potentially incestuous relationship. Virginia never denied her sexual liaisons with several men, two of whom testified that she had asked them to 'get rid' of Norman. It was clear that whatever their relationship was in public, Norman was unable to control his headstrong and hard-partying wife. Some of the testimonies only came to light when these men of low character asked to be paid to testify, making them barely credible.

No friends to testify on Virginia's behalf

With the public salivating upon every salacious fact, it was fair to say that Virginia and Jason Larzelere were convicted in the court of public opinion before the jury delivered its 5-7 guilty verdict for Virginia. Jason was subsequently acquitted due to the flimsy evidence by a disgruntled employee (Heidle) being the sole evidence in the case. Subsequent hearings brought to light the fact that the lone gunman that fateful day was not Jason, as Heidle had conveniently framed him for the murder. As Heidle had been given immunity from prosecution, many speculate that he tainted the stories about Virginia to protect himself and that it was he who murdered Larzelere. He committed suicide in 1999.

The allegations that Virginia was the mastermind who had her husband killed in cold blood to collect on his significant life insurance were presented but never successfully refuted. Her defence lawyer did not call any witness to the stand to testify on her behalf. A lifetime of alienation from meaningful relationships robbed her of this comfort. Her childhood of abuse and neglect impaired her ability to make and sustain meaningful and enduring friendships.

Her death sentence was overturned in 2008 though she remains incarcerated in the Homestead Correctional Institution, a 65-year-old widow, and she still maintains her innocence.

BLACK WIDOW BETTY LOU BEETS

ALICE WATERS

Betty Lou Beets is a perfect historical example of how multifaceted crime can be, how a victim could become an aggressor, or an aggressor may adopt the mask of victimhood, and how all is not necessarily as it seems. Convicted for murdering two men and assaulting or attempting to kill four, Betty Lou's story is one that would send chills down the spine of any man from any era. Only the fourth woman to be executed for murder, despite the overall statistics hovering around forty to fifty cases of capital punishment per year, her crimes were too gruesome and cold for the court to offer her a lesser sentence... or were they? As we shall see when we delve into her history, despite Betty Lou's extensive criminal record and constant charges against her from ex husbands and her own children, the justice system was eager to give her a way out of the death sentence and allow her to live her natural life out in prison. And although there were some mitigating circumstances, it is telling that Betty Lou Beets almost got away with a life sentence in a situation where many others would have been executed without remorse.

Betty Lou Beets was born Betty Lou Dunevant on the 12th of March 1937, in Roxboro, North Carolina, USA. Her parents were initially tobacco farmers, whose main pleasure in life was alcohol, resulting in rampant alcoholism and a violent family life not atypical of the rural poor of the Great Depression. They lived on a diet of salt pork and various flours, barely touching vegetables or fruit, let alone eggs, fish, nuts or pulses, essential for developing a healthy brain and body. Furthermore, Betty Lou was disabled. She was not completely deaf, but hard of hearing due to having contracted the measles some time between the ages of three and six. Her fever was so severe and prolonged that she suffered damage to her brain and ears. As her hearing was affected at such a young age, she suffered an impairment to her speech similar to what many deaf or hard of hearing children suffer. At another time, or in another family, Betty Lou may have received treatment and hearing aids, but as a poor family in 1940, they could not afford to get her the treatment she would have needed to hear and speak normally. Her education was strongly impacted as she could not learn to read or study, resulting in borderline illiteracy and innumeracy and a frustrating life at home and away. Betty Lou also claimed she had been raped by her father in early childhood, as well as sexually abused by others. By the age of twelve her family life was falling apart. Her mother had been institutionalized due to breakdowns caused by alcoholism and Betty Lou had to drop out of school so she could care for her younger brother and sister. Her father, who seemed to see her as a surrogate mother for her siblings, became guarded against any sign of Betty Lou escaping and would beat her for not taking full responsibility for her siblings. She was often at the doctor's office or in hospital for the injuries he inflicted on her. She finally left school completely. The family moved to Hampton, Virginia, while Betty Lou was still a young girl, so that her father could work as a machinist. They were poor, she was young and disabled and she was a victim at the hands of the very people who were supposed to care for her. These circumstances were hardly the healthiest for the young girl to grow up in, and it is not shocking that Betty Lou became increasingly unstable and inclined to criminality in such an environment during such a time of deprivation. However it is also noteworthy that many more people suffered equal or worse hardship, yet did not turn to criminal activity. Perhaps it was the combination of everything, all together at once, but as she grew up something was going very, very wrong inside Betty Lou.

At the age of fifteen she married her first husband, Robert Franklin Branson. Far from an age where anyone feels quite ready to move into adulthood, Betty Lou was married for the first time. She would remain with him for seventeen years before finally divorcing. Although she levied accusations of violence against all her husbands, Robert Franklin Branson was the only one whose life she did not threaten directly herself. It appears he picked up where her father left off. If she was ever a unilateral victim, this may have been the one time. Within the first year she attempted suicide and became pregnant. They had a daughter together. She also later had a son with Robert Branson, who was also named Robert after his father. They went onto have four more children. Their children may have been a factor in reducing the marital violence, extending the duration of the relationship and, ultimately, saving Robert Branson Senior's life. In 1958 he evicted her from their home and put her on a bus to Virginia while he kept her children, at which point Betty again attempted suicide via an overdose of sleeping pills. They divorced in 1969, which left Betty Lou a financial and emotional wreck.

Being single took its toll on Betty Lou. She attached her self-worth to her ability to stay married. She began drinking to fight her feelings of loneliness. Between her own insecurities and the hard time she had getting money from either Robert Branson or the Welfare service to support her, Betty Lou soon felt she needed to remarry. She married Billy York Lane at the age of thirty two. Their marriage was a tumultuous one, and very short. There was evidence of mutual violence and disregard for each other's wellbeing. Lane had been abusive towards a previous partner and Betty Lou responded to his violence in turn. Her daughters recall how he used to beat her senseless and how she used to attack him. He initially wanted to charge her for attempted murder, but swiftly dropped the charges after he was forced to admit he had attacked her, broken her nose and threatened her life. They divorced the same year and remarried again shortly after the trial.

After Betty Lou shot at him, Billy York Lane divorced her again, only a month after their remarriage, this time for good. It would prove the wisest decision of his life, as her subsequent husbands found out.

Betty Lou remained single for a year and unmarried for eight more years. During the interim Betty Lou worked in a warehouse, then took up work at a topless bar to cover the bills. She sent two of their children back home to Branson, as she could not afford to care for them. She went on to marry Ronnie C. Threlkold, her boyfriend of seven years, at the age of forty. However this relationship would be as unpredictable, violent and dangerous for Ronnie as it was for Billy. In this case there was little evidence Ronnie had been violent towards Betty Lou, although she accused him of violence at later dates, but her habits had been firmly cemented and she continued to display abusive behaviour towards him. She also continued to work at the topless bar, resulting in arrests and thirty days in country jail under the charge of public lewdness. Despite their seven year courtship, the marriage lasted just a year, culminating in Betty Lou Beets's attempted homicide of Ronnie in 1978, where she shot him in the stomach, wounding him, and their divorce in 1979.

She married Doyle Wayne Barker at the age of forty one, closely after her divorce from Threlkold. Their marriage lasted a mere seven weeks before her violent behaviour drove Doyle away from her. However his own violence was undeniable. He had stalked her, assaulted her and raped her during their short relationship. The day he left Betty Lou had bruises all over her face, neck, arms and chest. There is no available record of the divorce, however all living parties assumed it had taken place. However Doyle Wayne did not get out of their marriage unscathed. He disappeared after their divorce and his body was found years later, buried under a garage, killed by three gunshots.

But this grisly deed was not uncovered for many more years to come. Rather, Betty Lou went on to marry a firefighter named Jimmy Don Beets, her final husband, at the age of forty four.

"Jimmy Don Beets was a wonderful man," said a family friend. "He was loved by so many people. An old country boy that a lot people had respect for."

Their courtship would last a mere six months. Betty Lou would meet Jimmy while she worked as a waitress and the seduction began. Her two sons moved in with them. This would be her final marriage, and her actions within it would be her undoing. Although their courtship had been pleasant, they both suffered from alcoholism, which slowly drove their marriage to the same violence she had experienced previously. Less than a year later she murdered him by gunshot, and this time she was caught. Robert Branson, her son from her first marriage, had been informed that she intended to kill her last husband, telling him to steer clear of the residence as the murder took place. On the 6th of August 1983, Robert Branson Junior left their home and Betty Lou Beets committed the gruesome act. Not only did Robert provide evidence that the act was premeditated, but he also was expected to participate. Two hours after leaving the house, Robert Branson Junior returned, finding his step father dead with two gunshot wounds in his body. Rather than seek assistance, Robert Branson Junior, either tainted by a lifetime with a mother who viewed abuse and murder as daily events or himself an individual with low empathy, helped his mother to dispose of the body. Betty Lou Beets and Robert Branson Junior carted Jimmy Don Beets' body outside to an ornamental wishing well that stood in the front yard of their house. Undetected, they cast the body inside.

Then, Betty Lou returned to the house to cover up her acts. She called the police to report her husband missing from their Cedar Creek Lake home. The next day, Betty Lou became more devious. Perhaps inspired, perhaps unnerved by her success killing Doyle Wayne Barker, she realized she needed to create a story with which to divert the police from her trail. Robert Branson Junior recalled to the press how she had taken some of Jimmy Don Beets's heart medication down to his boat at the lake. Then she had removed the propeller, placed the medication in the boat and abandoned it, floating loosely in the water. Later that day, as the twenty four hours since Jimmy Don Beets's initial disappearance drew to a close, various officials began the search for the presumably missing man. Officers from the Henderson County Sheriff's department, various members of the fire department, as well as agents from the Texas Parks and Wildlife department searched for three weeks. They naturally found no body. However they did find Jimmy Don Beets's boat drifting in the lake, near to the Redwood Beach Marina. There they found his fishing license, an unused life jacket and the heart medication which Betty Lou Beets had placed there. Not knowing anything about the murder or the forged evidence, they brought Betty Lou Beets to the Marina as the sole witness, where she identified the boat and its contents as those of her husband. Although no body had been recovered, it was considered case closed.

Betty Lou Beets would have likely got away with both murders, were it not for confidential information given to the Henderson County Sheriff's Department two years later. The information suggested that Jimmy Don Beets had not disappeared innocently, and that his assumed death, with no body that had been found, may be the result of foul play. The evidence was enough that the cold case was reopened in Spring 1985. As their suspicions became stronger, the investigators were drawn to Betty Lou Beets, who was arrested on the 8th of June of 1985 and then booked into the Henderson County Jail. An officer on the case, Rick Rose, who had been in charge of her arrest warrant, secured a further warrant to search the Beets's home and lands, including the yard. Ultimately, they discovered Jimmy Don Beets's remains buried under the wishing well where he had been left two years prior. But another discovery would surface that would further disturb the case. Also in the back yard was a storage shed which could be moved. When the officers moved it, something compelled them to disturb the soil that had lain there several years. Perhaps it

was some confidential evidence or perhaps it was just intuition, but it
paid off when they discovered a second body. Doyle Wayne Barker, still
missing, was buried there, with three bullets in his body. All five bullets
matched the .38 caliber pistol which had been seized from their home
after another incident of Betty Lou's violent outbursts. Thanks to the
calls she had made the very day of his disappearance there was no room
to argue that she had been abusing drugs or alcohol at the time, but
there had been no physical evidence that suggested to detectives at the
time that Jimmy Don had been abusing her when the incident took
place. Her position was weak.

Faced with the evidence, Robert Branson Junior and his sister
Shirley finally confessed to their awareness of the killings, as well as
their hand in the crimes that had taken place. Not only had Betty
Lou told her son about the murder, but she had also informed her
daughter, by the Shirley Stegner and not living at the family home,
that she planned on killing her husband. Shirley was motivated by her
confession to also confess to her involvement in another crime. She
told the detectives that she had been involved in the burial of Doyle
Wayne Barker's body in October of 1981 after Betty Lou had shot him
to death.

In an effort to make herself more likeable to the jury, Betty Lou
Beets raised her history of domestic violence as an excuse for her
violent behaviour, levying charges against all her prior husbands, as
well as her father. However, this would be the first that anyone had
heard of most of these charges. This may have been due to attitudes of
the times, a desire to protect her children, or the apparently two-sided
nature of most of these incidents, however the jury would not believe
her claims. They were just too convenient. Instead, it was clear to them
that Betty Lou Beets was an unstable and dangerous woman and the
only connection between the five men she married and their violence.
Whatever the situation was, her psychological well being was never
considered during the trial. Despite the obvious impact her upbringing

and life would have on her mental state and the fact that her actions up until that point were indicative of definite mental illness, the trial system of the time did not account for that.

Furthermore, the premeditated nature of her actions was evident through her children's abundant testimonials, where they confessed she had shared her intent to kill not only the husbands she managed to murder, but that she had expressed a desire to kill all the men she had been married to. Not only that, but her success concealing the bodies, under the wishing well and under the garden shed, showed a lack of remorse and serious consideration of her crimes. However it seems Betty Lou had not been as careful as she thought. As soon as the trial began, various other witnesses emerged to testify against her. Various people recalled her attempting to collect life insurance of over a hundred thousand dollars as well as a pension of over a thousand dollars a month after Jimmy Don's declared death. A year after the official death of Jimmy Don Beets, she successfully sold his boat, the primary evidence that he had disappeared. She claimed she did not know about his pension or insurance, however seeing as Jimmy Don Beets was already retired and claiming his pension, this claim fell short. Furthermore, had she no awareness of them she would not have pursued either so actively. She claimed she had been told about them when she visited an attorney by the name or E. Ray Andrews about a fire insurance claim she needed to make, at which point he discovered she could claim his insurance and pension. However her own filing for these benefits did not align with the supposed visit, and the only person who could say for sure that she had not known about her deceased husband's finances was E. Ray Andrews himself, who agreed to represent her in exchange for the rights to book and movie deals concerning her life and case.

Betty Lou Beets was indicted for murder for remuneration or the promise of remuneration, with her recovery of his life insurance and pension as evidence. She plead not guilty and was taken to trial, where she was found guilty of the capital offence of first degree murder on the 11th of October of 1985. She was found again guilty during a hearing on the 14th of October 1985 and was sentenced to death by the trial court. This was due to her prior history of violence and attempted murders, which suggested that she would present a threat to others in the future, specifically to any man who entered a relationship with her again. Yet her conviction and sentence were quickly and successfully appealed to the Texas Court of Criminal Appeals. Such was the situation that, under Texas law, crime for the sake of insurance and pension claims was not covered by the definition of "murder for remuneration", instead falling into two separate categories of first degree murder and insurance fraud, or crime with intent to commit insurance fraud. The Texas Court of Criminal Appeals reversed her conviction for capital murder, citing the Texas Penal Code as evidence that her particular case could not be filed as "murder for remuneration". The State then requested a rehearing of the cause. Although her original conviction had been overturned, the fact remained that Betty Lou Beets was guilty of homicide under some circumstance or another.

On the 21st of September of 1988, the Court of Criminal Appeals reinstated her conviction and sentence based on the evidence received. Betty Lou Beets was on death row. Her execution was scheduled for the 8th of November 1989.

However her court case did not go as it should have in the first place. Attorney E. Ray Andrews was heavily invested in sensationalizing her case as much as he could, seeing as he would profit enormously from the case blowing up into a media phenomenon. So although she claimed and he later agreed that she had known nothing of her husband's finances, the trial was conducted under the assumption that she was fully aware of the money she would receive. Not only that, but E. Ray Andrews did everything in his power to create a more dramatic case on both sides, which ultimately meant excluding Betty Lou from much of the information about her own trial. Betty Lou was becoming desperate at this point. Although she had a long history of domestic violence, attempted murder and two bodies in her garden, she decided to attempt to blame the murder of Jimmy Don Beets on Robert Branson Junior, her own son. She did not seem to have made the statement in sound mind, but E. Ray Andrews allowed her to speak on her own behalf and did not retract it, as it added dramatic quality to the event. He tried to cover up later, saying that Betty Lou had possibly been taking the blame for her son, however he had no proof other than that Robert Branson Junior was male and from a rough background. This statement and its acceptance horrified the court, as it was alarming to them to see a mother who, rather than protect her children, was willing to throw them under the bus by falsely accusing them of a crime she had more than evidently committed. Furthermore, by admitting and adhering to the story that Robert Branson Junior was in fact the actual killer, Betty Lou lost all chances of arguing that she acted in self-defence and made her own accusations of domestic violence against Jimmy Don and her prior husbands completely irrelevant. This is despite the fact that a leading domestic violence specialist of the time believed Betty Lou Beets had been significantly mentally impacted by her experiences, and that she suffered "the emotional, cognitive, and behavioural components of battered woman syndrome, rape trauma syndrome, and PTSD" which he added must have interacted with her pre-existing organic brain damage from her childhood illness, history of battering and substance abuse. All together, this would have presented a robust case for her mental illness and need for treatment rather than punishment. However E. Ray Andrews discarded this option in favour of the more dramatic choice of supporting Betty Lou's accusation against her son. They became stuck in the position of having to argue she did not kill her husband at all. This context may have reduced her sentence, or made her eligible to claim insanity. However neither of these options were available.

Throughout the entire case, E. Ray Andrews failed to represent her seriously and did nothing to prevent her from shooting herself in the foot repeatedly. In fact, seeing the case was a lost cause and that he stood to gain more from her sentence than her freedom, Andrews began drinking heavily for the duration of the trial. He chose not to bear witness to her claims that she did not know about Jimmy Don Beets's pension or insurance, which would have transformed the case to one of murder in the context of domestic violence, rather than murder for remuneration. He managed to offer the jury no reasons to consider that Betty Lou was not a serious threat to those around her, eventually sealing her fate. Yet he remained her attorney for the duration of her appeal as well. It was he who raised the point that her financial gain was not necessarily the motivator for murder, but a by product. He also finally raised that she was not aware of the insurance or pension until she spoke to him, however this was met with scepticism due to his negligence to mention it any sooner, and was perceived as a lie in effort to overturn Betty Lou's criminal charges after his initial failure to protect her.

On the 16th of October 1989, Betty Lou filed a motion called a stay of execution which would delay her execution to give her time to prepare and file a habeas corpus application with the state. On the 1st of November she filed the application and the trial court delayed her execution so that the claims she was raising, such as consideration towards her mental state and marital conditions, could be properly addressed. During this time Betty Lou wrote several letters from prison in which she attempted to defend her good name and that of her last husband. She attempted to balance the accusations that she was a black widow by reminding the court that she was Jimmy Don's fourth wife as well. However his previous wives did not come forward to support her. She also defended her own identity, denying that she ever worked as a barmaid, regardless of her own charges for lewd behaviour, and that she was never on welfare, despite her claims after her first divorce. She also said that the Fire Department Chaplain, who stated he had informed her about Beets's insurance and pension, had spoken to her sister in law, Betty Beets, instead. She even quibbled over the descriptions of her garden, insisting the well was a planter in the shape of a well and not an actual well. It was clear that Betty Lou Beets was desperate to save face and project a more pleasant, more ordinary identity than the one which E. Ray Andrews had created for her in the courtroom. It was also clear that her mental health was degrading as she endured life in prison and submitted her habeas corpus petition. In her petition she argued against her sentence of the death penalty, raising issues such as the alleged value Jimmy Don Beets apparently added the community, the testimonials of victims and sufferers whose statements were unconstitutional under the Victim Impact Statements act of 1987, and the poor assistance which E. Ray Andrews provided, especially regarding her history of domestic abuse. Yet without his help in writing and presenting the letter, her claims were weak and not fully backed by legal evidence. Andrews did not visit her from the point of her sentencing and prepared for her trials without ever speaking to her. Furthermore, she could have claimed that his services were provided against American Bar Association rules, which prohibit the trade of legal services for copyright issues, such as the rights to her case. None of this was raised by her against him, and as such it was not considered during her habeas corpus appeal.

However on the 27th of June her appeal for state habeas corpus was turned away. She was placed in the position of proving that, had E. Ray Andrews presented a testimony about her lack of awareness of the insurance and her history of domestic violence, the jury would have judged her not guilty of a capital crime. Without a proper attorney to defend her, it would be impossible for Betty Lou to prove this was the case, and the court deemed Andrews's mistakes to have been harmless to her trial. The Fifth Circuit Court of Appeals went on to turn down her final appeals. The judges remained convinced that, regardless of any remaining evidence, Betty Lou Beets's history of violence and attempted murder, along with the two concealed bodies in her garden, were evidence enough that a death sentence was a fair response to the crime that had taken place. She had displayed violence her whole life, even towards men who had not presented a threat to her, and had attempted to kill all but one of her husbands. She had concealed her murders carefully and for many years and was willing to place the blame on her own adult son. In other words, regardless of her own situation, her criminal intent was viewed as evident and incorrigible, and her death sentence was the only fitting end to her crime spree.

On death row, Betty Lou Beets retained some supporters, mostly her own children. Some of Betty Lou's daughters went to E. Ray Andrews with photographic evidence of the domestic abuse she had suffered in order to request a parole review, but were declined. They insisted on presenting the evidence that she had suffered and that her acts of violence were a result of brain damage and abuse, not of malicious intent. Faye Lane, one of her daughters, insisted that her mother would only have done anything so horrific if she believed she was abused. Domestic violence awareness groups and charities acting against the death sentence appealed to have her sentence changed to a life sentence in prison, based not only on her own suffering, but on their universal stance against the irreversible process of the death penalty. Yet even those defending her maintained that she was a violent, unpredictable woman and not safe to exit into the general public.

And not all her children were so kind. Shirley told the press that Doyle Wayne Barker was killed because he owned the trailer where they lived, and that after the divorce which Barker had initiated, Betty Lou and her children would be evicted from the trailer and left homeless. This set a precedent where even her own daughter could not believe that Betty Lou was completely unaware of the financial benefits of murdering Jimmy Don Beets, especially not after she had successfully killed Barker. Knowing that she was still doubted and seeing hope as ever distant, Betty Lou composed her memoirs from death row, presenting her case.

Beets turned to her last resort which was to appeal to then-governor George W. Bush to spare her life. After a media incident where he jokingly insulted the last woman to be executed in Texas in an insensitive manner, George W. Bush seemed keen to prove he had no bias against women, even in the prison system, and agreed to review her case. This would have meant hearing the witnesses which had not been heard by the trial lawyer and present a case against her execution based on the circumstances of her life, including medical and psychiatric evidence. He could have granted her a thirty day reprieve in which he made his decision, however this never materialized. His number was made available and he received thousands of calls and letters from people urging him to spare her, with only fifty seven endorsing her sentence. Yet he did not grant the reprieve or halt the execution.

Betty Lou Beets was finally executed on the 24th of February of 2000, via lethal injection. Protestors from various organisations gathered outside as her sentence awaited. She declined both her last meal and her final statement, having been given by then enough time to make sense of what was happening and to say everything which needed to be said. Strapped to the death chamber gurney, she received her injection at six pm and died within eighteen minutes. She was sixty two years old. She left behind five adult children, nine grandchildren and six great-grandchildren, as well as her memoirs. Her story may be shocking, and it may be hard to pick sides at times, but that is exactly why her trial presents a solid case against the black and white ideals the court system held regarding crime and punishment, perpetrator and victim, defence and offence. Someone can at once be a victim of horrific crimes and a perpetrator of them, at once be a defendant and raise accusations, at once deserve punishment yet suffer a crime gone unpunished. There is no doubt that Betty Lou Beets was a violent woman who invited violence into her own life, an alcoholic and a murderer. However there is no doubt either that she was a good mother within her capacity, a victim of a series of horrific crimes, a disabled person with a background she could not escape and a desperate woman who saw no way out of her situation. Neither black nor white, good not bad, Betty Lou Beets sits in the grey areas of the law.

BLACK WIDOW JANIE LOU GIBBS

JANE CARLISLE

Janie Lou Hickox was born on December 25th, Christmas day, 1932 in Cordele, Georgia. Cordele is now a town with just over 11 000 residents, and is proudly known as the Watermelon Capital of the World. The city is named after Cordelia Hawkins who was the eldest daughter of Colonel Samuel Hawkins, the president of the Savannah, Americus and Montgomery Railway. In November of 1864, the area temporarily served as the capital of Georgia, but Cordele as it is now knows was founded in 1888 as a junction between two major railroads: the Savannah, Americus and Montgomery line and the Georgia Southern and Florida. Notable people from the area include jazz and blues singers, sportsmen, a White House Press Secretary and the president of an international Christian TV network. Nobody suspected that a serial killer who would be a black widow was growing up in their midst.

There is not much information about Janie's upbringing, but it was strictly religious and she grew up in a fairly poor family. Janie was married to Charles Clayton Gibbs, a farmer, when she was only fifteen. The two moved to the nearby town of Arabi which was just under ten miles away from Cordele, a mere fifteen minutes by car. Both of these towns fall under the Crisp County district. Arabi now has a population of 586, with 185 hosueholds and 125 families living in the town. Janie and Charles were regular churchgoers, and they had three boys: Roger Ludean Gibbs, Melvin Watess Gibbs, and Marvin Ronald Gibbs. For eighteen years, they lived quiet and devoted lives on the farm until tragedy began to take blow after blow upon the family.

Janie was known for spending all of her spare time helping out at the church and for her day-care service that she ran in her home for children of working mothers. Accounts note that on most days Janie would have around twenty-five children at her house aside from her own sons. While some believed her to have almost fanatic religious beliefs, all members of Janie's church and community believed her to be sound of mind and to know the difference between right and wrong, testimonies that they would later make in the investigation. Nobody felt that Janie had any emotional or mental issues, and simply knew her as a devoted mother who held God and the church close to her heart. When she wasn't looking after children in the community, Janie was helping out with events around the church and other ways to support the congregation.

Just before the tragedies began to occur, Janie had travelled to Albany, Georgia for a doctor's appointment. There she had been diagnosed with Lou Gehrig's disease, a motor neurone disease that destroys muscle control, is also known as amyotrophic lateral sclerosis or ALS. The disease progresses from a stiffness of muscles to twitching while the person becomes increasingly weaker. Eventually, once their muscles have decreased in size enough, the patient has trouble with speaking, swallowing, and eventually breathing. Janie was very aware that her body would begin to systematically shut itself down. After her trial, her defense lawyer Frank Martin stated that this was one of the most tragic aspects of the case as far as he was concerned. Frank believed that due to Janie's acute awareness of how her illness would progress paired with her fanatic religious beliefs, she wanted everybody that was close to her in the world to go to heaven so that she would be with them when she finally passed. Although Janie never admitted this in court, the murder of her husband, three sons, and grandson, all of whom she loved dearly, suggests that this might have been a contributing factor to the decisions or delirium that ended in her intentionally poisoning five members of her family.

The first member of the family to go was her husband, Charles Clayton Gibbs, who died on the 21st January 1966 when he was only thirty-nine years old. Janie was an avid cook, and she always had home cooked meals ready for her family when they returned home from work or school. After having had one such meal, Charles collapsed in the family home and was taken to hospital. Janie went to the hospital to care for him and brought a flask of soup with her. After Charles was served this final meal, he died painfully from stomach cramps and convulsions. Years later, investigators realized that this soup must have been laced with a particularly strong dose of arsenic from rat poison that Janie had been giving him in trace amount in his meals and coffees.

When administered in small amounts like this, it can be very difficult to determine if somebody is a victim of arsenic poisoning unless a doctor thinks to specifically check for it. Arsenic poisoning can result in a host of different symptoms and organ failures, so it is often the case that medical professionals are waiting for more evidence to be able to provide a solid diagnosis while the victim continues to be poisoned by somebody close to them. Symptoms can include abdominal pain and cramping, diarrhea, vomiting, dark urine, dehydration, vertigo, delirium, shock, hair loss, and convulsions. Arsenic is flavorless and odorless, making it very difficult for somebody to connect their normal food and beverage consumption with their illness. Arsenic poisoning can affect the skin, liver, lungs, and kidneys, which is both why it is such a potentially fatal condition and why it is difficult to detect without a hunch. In the case of Charles, his death was written down to an undiagnosed liver disease that he had been suffering for some time. While the doctors wanted to perform an autopsy on her husband to be sure, Janie said that she didn't want him 'all cut up', and her wishes were respected.

The church community provided an overwhelming amount of support for the Gibbs family once Charles had passed. The entire congregation was shocked, Charles having seemed to be in such good health until recent times, and also because he was still so young. The Gibbs family were provided with company, meals, emotional support, and everything that the members of their church community could possibly extend. When the life insurance claim for Charles came through, Janie donated a significant portion of these funds to the church to demonstrate her thanks for everything that they had done and her belief in the community. Janie claimed that she and the boys would have to continue on as best they could, and that she felt that with the strength of the church community behind them they would be able to make it through. Even after their home burned down soon after Charles' death and the family moved back to Janie's home town of Cordele, Janie continued to offer day-care services for the children of working mothers. There has never been an investigation into the house burning down, but the timing is certainly curious. Is it possible that Janie felt this was the only way to justify moving her family back to her home town of Cordele? It is clear from the rest of her actions over this two year period that she wasn't thinking rationally, and perhaps she wanted to escape the physical environment where she had been married for all of those years. Whatever the reason, just as nobody suspected that Janie had anything to do with the death of her husband, there was no investigation into whether or not the house burned down due to arson.

It was around this time that the oldest Gibbs son Roger took notice of a girl in their congregation, Ellen Penny. A relationship began to blossom between them under the watchful eye of Janie. The two teenagers began to spend more and more time together at church events, and participated in the same activities together. If Roger was assigned the duty of retrieving the bibles at the end of a ceremony, Ellen would always be there too help him. Very soon the two began to date. Over the next year Roger and Ellen married and she became pregnant with their first child. Ellen began living at the Gibb's residence, but this relationship and pregnancy was against a dark backdrop. It is difficult to say whether Janie took an immediate dislike to Ellen, or whether she did not want her son getting married and having a child so early like she had herself. Perhaps she wanted a different life for him, or harbored some resentment on being married off at such a young age. Either way, Janie never had a good relationship with Ellen and many times would behave as if she almost didn't register her existence.

Only months after Charles' death, Marvin began to develop the same symptoms as his father had. Having moved house and town, perhaps the rest of the family felt a separation with losing their father and like this wouldn't happen again with their youngest brother. There are no records of comments from the brothers or the community being concerned that Marvin would go the same way as his father, but sure enough, nine months after his father had died, Marvin Ronald Gibbs died on the 29th August 1966. Marvin too was determined to have an undiagnosed liver disease just like his father had, and Janie once again refused to have an autopsy performed. Perhaps Janie felt that performing an autopsy was an ungodly act that would in some way affect the chances of her family members getting into heaven? While the largest reason was most certainly to protect her own interests and for her to be able to complete her task, autopsy is a process rejected by many faiths and traditions. The police and staff at the insurance company pushed for autopsies as they felt that two deaths of this nature so close together and in one family didn't make sense. At this time, some members of the church community began to have suspicions about the deaths in the Gibbs family, but nobody wanted to be the one to come forward and accuse the pious and highly involved church member that Janie was. For many, there was still a huge disconnect. So even though the insurance company and the police of Crisp County were pressing for an autopsy on the body of young Marvin, Janie still had the support of the community enough to request that this procedure not be undertaken. Despite their suspicions, many in the community still felt that Janie wouldn't be capable of doing such a thing, particularly when it was to her own family that she seemed to have such an active devotion to.

Once again the church community poured support for the Gibb's family, offering counsel and companionship for Janie and her two remaining boys. When Marvin's life insurance came through, Janie once again provided a large portion of this claim to the church, which was undergoing significant renovations. While some began to talk about Janie seeming to almost be enjoying her new lifestyle, never being seen in the same dress and buying a new car, they could not help notice how generous she was also being with these funds. Those members of the community who still had faith in Janie chalked this spending down to a way to cope with her losses. However, Ellen Penny remained highly suspicious of Janie Gibbs. She didn't know how to speak out about her, both because she needed to live with the family and because she was so young, but after Marvin's death Ellen was certain that what was happening to the Gibbs family was no random or hereditary tragedy. Then, Melvin also began to fall ill.

As Melvin (often referred to in some articles as Lester) began to follow the path of his father and younger brother, the sixteen year old started to experience dizzy spells. Some people in the community attributed these headaches to puberty as the boy was sixteen. By this point, with such serious difficulties in the family, it is a wonder that Melvin's complaints weren't taken more seriously. He went downhill sharply. The doctors, not wanting to claim his death as another bout of undiagnosed liver disease that they weren't certain of, labeled his death a result of hepatitis. Once again a claim was made for life insurance, a portion donated to the church, and support lavished upon the Gibbs' family. At this point, Ellen became terrified for the life of her husband, herself, and their unborn child.

About a month after Melvin's death, Ellen and Roger's baby, Raymond, was born. Everybody noticed that Janie's mood lifted, and the community felt that this is where the horror ended for the Gibb's family. Janie was thrilled with her grandson, even though she had been so early married herself and her son had had his first child so early, making Janie a grandmother at thirty-four. Janie often used to show the baby to anybody who came around to the house, and would often be seen out with Raymond around the city. Ellen began to feel at ease around this time as Janie seemed to have changed entirely. The way that she interacted with Ellen seemed to have improved, and it seemed that the way that Janie went about all of her daily tasks with a different air.

However, even the baby began to fall ill soon. Ellen was in a state of desperation and didn't know what to do, the child only being one month old. The young girl has nobody that she could turn to, and didn't feel confident enough to make an accusation against Janie, even to her own husband. Despite the fact that Raymond was perfectly healthy, he died of an apparent heart condition. Everybody who was close to the Gibbs were completely shocked to hear of Raymond's death, and this is the point that many members of the congregation became highly suspicious of Janie. However, nobody did anything to prevent her from claiming the fifth and final member of her immediate family, her eldest and grieving son, with both Roger and Ellen still living with her at the time.

In the weeks after their baby died, Roger began to fall ill. Ellen, who was still under twenty at this age, had still not found the courage or the means to speak out against Janie. This may have been due to her living situation, or perhaps due to the sudden death of her son, but as Roger grew increasingly ill Ellen could do nothing but watch him deteriorate. She notes that during this time her husband constantly had red eyes, had visible rings around these, and was always pale and lacking in energy. He also used to get very severe headaches, but wasn't the type of person that liked to talk about any suffering that he was experiencing. The most that he would discuss these headaches was when he would be in such pain that he would be flinching. Ellen would ask if his head was giving him trouble again, to which he would respond with short and basic answers. Roger eventually found himself bedridden, being cared for by his mother. Despite what had happened to his father, two brothers, and own son, Roger never shared any suspicions about his mother with Ellen. It is entirely possible that he had figured out what was going on, being the last left, but didn't know how to get himself out of the situation.

Over the weeks, Roger's health got worse and worse. Ellen remembers overhearing an argument between Roger and his mother where he was repeatedly saying

"You did it! You did this to me!"

He was saying it over and over again as fiercely as he was able to in his deteriorated state. Ellen did not fully understand the conversation as she made sure that she kept out of sight. She asked Roger about it later in private, but he didn't reveal anything further and simply said that he and his mother had been squabbling over something. Ellen began to wonder whether she was paranoid about the situation, but it seemed that everything was pointing towards Janie's involvement in not only Roger's sickness but the suspicious deaths of the other four. Ellen stayed by her husband and cared for him as best she could, watching on as Janie nursed her son.

When Roger was eventually placed in hospital, Janie and Ellen spent nearly all of their time there. After a couple of days, Ellen noticed that Janie was in the habit of taking the water jug that the hospital placed in their room, tipping it down the sink, and replacing it with her own water. When Ellen asked her why she was doing this, Janie claimed that the hospital water had too much sulfur and that it hurt his throat. It was later realized that she was feeding her last remaining immediate family member increasing doses of arsenic through the water. Janie forced Roger to drink the water in large gulps and often. Once again, it is difficult to understand why this behavior was accepted by nurses, and also why nobody gave Roger testing for arsenic poisoning when four members of his family had died so suspiciously. However, even though this was a fairly common way for women to kill at the time, it is not until later years that we realized the signs and hints that might have saved the Gibbs family from their wife and mother.

One day, Janie asked Ellen to give Roger some water. Janie filled up a tall glass and placed it in Ellen's hand. Ellen gave Roger a small sip, but Janie demanded that he finish the whole glass, telling her that his throat is dry and he needs more. Ellen tipped the whole glass of water down her husband's throat, unknowingly giving him the final and strongest dose of arsenic. Perhaps Janie had been hoping that the blame might be placed on Ellen, or maybe she got satisfaction out of Ellen being the one that finally killed Roger, Janie having never been too keen on the girl. As Janie didn't want an autopsy on Roger, just like it was for the others, it is hard to say whether this act was a final insurance in her mind of her not being guilty of the crime, or whether it was the latter and she got satisfaction out of Ellen killing her spouse unintentionally. It is also possible, with Roger being left for last, that she was the least willing to kill him and needed Ellen to perform this final duty. After all, it would have made sense to kill the older two sons first and leave the younger one in her care, Marvin being so young and the least able of all three brothers to be able to take any action against his mother even if he had figured out what was happening. This suggests that Roger might have been somewhat of a favorite of Janie's, and that she wanted as much time with him as she could. Whatever the reason, Roger died soon after receiving the dose. He was only nineteen, and this finished Janie's work, whether it was insurance fraud or what she perceived to be God's work.

Just as she had with her two younger sons and her husband, Janie attempted to stop medical professionals from undertaking autopsies on Roger and Raymond Gibbs. However, as Ellen was the wife and mother, she has the rights of next of kin. Autopsies were performed that revealed extremely high levels of arsenic in Roger's organs, around twenty times that which you would expect to find in a body during an autopsy where arsenic has not been the cause of death. It was at this time that the Crisp County police called for the bodies of Charles, Marvin, and Melvin to be exhumed. People crowded around at the graveyard to watch while the bodies were taken out of the ground and placed on blue tarps. People began to say that they had thought there was something suspicious the whole time. A lot of guilt began to spread through the community. What if they had mentioned something earlier? Would they have at least been able to save the lives of Roger and his infant son? Mothers who had given their children to Janie to look after day in and day out felt embarrassed about their judgment of her character. This time the sympathy poured out for young Ellen who has lost her home, husband, and baby all within the space of a month. All five murders were committed in a short period of time, between 1966 and 1967. In all, Janie had received $31 000 in life insurance payments and given around ten percent of this to the church, but now she would have to answer for the crimes that she had done against those in the world that trusted her the most. Eric Hickey who has performed a study on female serial killers including Janie Lou Gibbs in 1991 claims that "These are the *quiet killers*, every bit as lethal as male serial murderers, but we are seldom aware of one in our midst because of their low visibility." Hickey also found that it takes an average of eight years to catch a female serial killer, nearly double what it takes on average to identify and arrest male serial killers.

Janie was arrested on Christmas Eve 1967, the day before her thirty-fifth birthday. She admitted to having killed all five of her immediate family members, but claimed that she didn't have a motive for doing so. While many people claim that she did this for the insurance money, there is still the chance that she genuinely committed the crimes in the name of her fanatic religious beliefs, wanting her family to be with her in heaven.

By February, Janie was determined to be insane and not fit for a trial but it was still agreed that she should not be able to live out her life in the community as she had been before. Janie took up residence at a state mental hospital where she served as a hospital cook, living there until 1976. At this time, multiple people had testified that they thought Janie was aware enough of her actions that she should have to deal with their legal ramifications. On May 9th 1976, Janie was convicted for her crimes and handed down five life sentences, one for each family member that she had poisoned. Janie's sister came to visit her in an attempt to understand the things that Janie has done, but found that she was largely nonresponsive and bewildered. The first question that her sister asked was *Why did you kill your family, Janie?* To which Janie responded she didn't know. Her sister attempted again, saying *Do you feel guilty?* Janice once again responded that she didn't know, seeming to be removed and numbed to the situation. Her sister made one final attempt to reach out to Janie and understand what had happened, asking *Can I do anything to help you?* For the third time, Janie responded that she didn't know. Her sister continued to visit her in jail in an attempt to understand more about Janie, what she had done, and what she was going through. But it seemed that no matter how much she tried, Janie was like a shell of what she had previously been.

She came up for parole seventeen times but was denied on each occasion. In April of 1999, due to her failing health as a result of Parkinson's disease, Janie was released into her sister's care. The last years of her life were spent in a wheel chair at a nursing home in Douglasville, Georgia, where she died on February 7th 2010. She now rests in the Sunrise Memorial Gardens at Lithia Springs in Douglas County, Georgia.

BLACK WIDOW JUDY BUENOANO

ERIN CARTER

Judy Buenoano loved men. But she loved killing them more.

In 1971, she murdered her husband James and nine years later she would kill her own son, Michael. In 1983, she would attempt but fail to kill her boyfriend, John Gentry. She is also believed to have been responsible for the death of Bobby Joe Morris (another boyfriend) in 1978. She was never convicted of the Morris crime, however, as by the time the authorities had connected the dots she was sentenced to death for the murder of her first husband.

But the suspicions didn't stop with the Morris death. Buenoano is also suspected of killing a man in 1974 and in 1980, another boyfriend would die under suspicious circumstances.

Buenoano would become the first woman executed in Florida since 1848 and only the third woman executed since capital punishment had been reinstated in 1976.

She would be sent to the electric chair in 1998. Her last words were that she wanted to be remembered as a "good mother."

Instead, she would go down as one of the most sadistic female serial killers in American history.

This is her story.

EARLY LIFE

Judy was born Judias Welty in Quanah, Texas on April 4th, 1943. Her father was a day laborer at a local farm. Judy would talk about her mother being a full-blooded member of the Mesquite Apache tribe but little did she know that a "Mesquite Apache" tribe didn't exist.

Her mother would die of tuberculosis when Judy was only two years old. She and her baby brother Robert would be sent to live with their grandparents while their two older siblings would be put up for adoption.

"When Judy's mother died," forensic psychologist Paula Orange said. "It sent Judy's life into a tailspin. This is one of those 'Butterfly Effect' scenarios. A tragic circumstance that occurred early in a child's life that led to her perpetuating pain on everyone else for the rest of her own adult life."

She would eventually leave her grandparents and join her father in Roswell, New Mexico. He had remarried and Judy would claim that both he and her new stepmother would beat, starve, and burn her with cigarettes.

They made her a "house slave", forcing her to do chores around the house at their bidding. Judy would finally act out at the age of fourteen as she would burn two of her step brothers with hot grease. Not stopping there, she attacked both her father and step-mom with fists flying.

Police would be called and Judy would be jailed for over two months. After she served her jail time, the judge gave Judy a choice, either return home or go to reform school. She opted for the latter and was sent to Foothills High School. She would remain there until 1959 when she would graduate at the age of sixteen.

She held her entire family in contempt, particularly her younger brother Robert.

"I wouldn't spit down his throat if his guts were on fire," Judy once said when asked about her brother.

CHANGING IDENTITY

Judy returned to Roswell but changed her name to "Anna Schultz". She found work as a nurse aide and would give birth to a baby boy out of wedlock, Michael Schultz on March 30, 1961. Judy would remain silent on the identity of the baby's father but people believed that Judy was having an affair with a pilot from the nearby air force base.

In 1963, the twenty-two-year-old Judy would marry James Goodyear. Goodyear was twenty-nine years old and serving as a sergeant in the United States Air Force.

They would have their first child together, James Jr, four years later. James would celebrate the event by legally adopting Michael. Daughter Kimberly would come a year later as the family would move to Orlando, Florida.

Judy would then open her own business, starting the Conway Acres Child Care Center in Orlando. She listed James as the co-owner even though he was during a one-year tour in the Vietnam War. After returning home, he only had three months of downtime before he was admitted to the U.S. Naval Hospital in Orlando, complaining from symptoms staff physicians never quite identified. He would die on September 15, 1971.

Goodyear was only thirty-seven years old at the time of death and authorities believed he died due to natural causes.

"He came home from Vietnam ill and he never got well," Judy said. ``It had nothing to do with me. I was not in Vietnam."

"Crazy that Goodyear was able to survive the horrors of Vietnam but not Judy Buenoano," Orange said. "He had no idea he was married to a sociopath. She had no respect for the fact that he had just put himself on the line for her and the country. All she saw were dollar signs."

Judy poisoned James with arsenic and waited almost a week after his death before cashing in his three life insurance policies. A few months later, an "accidental fire" burned down their Orlando home. Judy would receive another $90,000 in fire insurance.

She lost her husband and her home. But her purse was never fatter.

NO GRIEVING WIDOWS ALLOWED

Judy would waste no time finding another man. Despite having three kids in tow, she would find a new love in Bobby Joe Morris when she moved her family to Pensacola.

It was business as usual for Judy as she had a fat bank account courtesy of James Goodyear and a new beau in Bobby Joe. Eldest son Michael, however, was not doing well in school. He scored on the low end on IQ tests and was a behavioral problem. Judy would get him evaluated at a state hospital in 1974 and then sent Michael out to foster care where he would also receive psychiatric treatment.

Judy's new home would suffer another "accidental fire" and she collected money from the insurance. She then took Michael out of foster care and moved to Trinidad, Colorado with Bobby Joe and the rest of her children. Judy then changed her name from "Anna Schultz" to "Judias Morris".

FOUR YEARS MAX

Judy would date Bobby Joe for four years before deciding it was time to cut him loose.

Bobby Joe would start to suffer from the same mysterious illness as James Goodyear did years earlier as he complained of dizziness and vomiting. He would be admitted to San Rafael Hospital on January 4, 1978, but doctors would not be able to pinpoint what was wrong with him. He would be sent home to Judy's care two weeks later. Two days later, however, he would would pitch face-first into his dinner plate, unconscious. He would be rushed to the hospital, but Judy knew that her "medicine" had taken effect.

Five days later, Bobby Joe Morris would be dead. Doctors would chalk up his death to cardiac arrest and metabolic acidosis.

Judy would wait, just like she did after she killed James, before cashing in on Bobby Joe's life insurance.

Authorities were none the wiser.

But Bobby Joe's family suspected something fishy was going on. Back in 1974, Judy and Bobby Joe had been visiting Brewton, Alabama when a man from Florida was found dead in a motel room in that town. Police would find the man in the room after receiving an anonymous call. He was shot in the chest with a .22-caliber weapon and his throat was cut open.

Judy's connection to the crime? Bobby Joe's mother had overheard Judy telling her son about the murder.

"The sonofabitch shouldn't have come up here in the first place," Judy said. "If he came up here he was gonna die."

Bobby Joe had told his mother about the crime on his deathbed. She thought the confession could be attributed to his delirium, but Bobby Joe told her too many specifics to ignore.

"We should never had done that terrible thing," Bobby Joe mumbled to his mother. "Never should have done that to him."

She tipped off police but they would not be able to find any fingerprints inside the room and no bullet was recovered from the corpse. The case remained unsolved.

WHAT'S ONE MORE SURNAME?

On May 3rd, 1978, Judy would change her name again. This go around, she would change her last name to Buenoano, which in Spanish meant "good year." She stated that she meant it as a tribute to her husband James Goodyear and her Apache mother.

Things continued to go bad with Michael as he dropped out of high school in the tenth grade. With limited employment opportunities, he would join the army in June of 1979 and get assigned to Ft. Benning in Georgia after basic training. When he was on his way to his new post, he visited Judy in Pensacola.

Judy greeted her son with open arms. Then she began poisoning him.

By the time he reached Ft. Benning, he felt sick. Army physicians would find seven times the normal level of arsenic in his body.

They could do little to reverse the damage done. Six weeks after his arrival, the muscles in his arms and legs and deteriorated to the point where he was a paraplegic.

"Michael had no use of his legs," Orange said. "And he could not move his arms past his elbow. Again, Judy was a sociopath. It is unfathomable for a normal human being, a mother, to do this to her own child. Yet she did it to Michael. He was always an inconvenience to her but now that he had military insurance he could become an asset in death."

Judy would give Michael the short shrift while favoring James and Kimberly. Michael and James didn't get along well as clearly their mother favored the latter. Judy would hide Michael when people came over because she was ashamed of him. She would have a neighbor named Constance Lang watch over him when visitors arrived.

"Michael didn't fit the picture Judy wanted to present to the world," Orange said. "She wanted to be looked at like a woman of high status. She drove a Corvette and owned her own business. Michael was a slow-thinking kid. She didn't want anyone to see that."

The army didn't investigate the reasons behind Michael's inordinate levels of arsenic. Instead, they set him up with leg braces and a prosthetic device on one of his arms.

He would be discharged from active duty because of the medical disability.

But his mother saw dollar signs.

The day after his return home, Judy wasted no time. She organized a fishing trip with Michael, James, and daughter Kimberly. They would leave Kimberly ashore at the East River bridge while they went into the water with a two-seat canoe. A small folding lawn chair had been placed in the middle of the canoe for Michael who had was outfitted with a leg brace, a fishing reel, and a ski belt.

James would state that had fished for about two hours when they were reaching shore when a "snake fell into the canoe." He said that everyone panicked as the snake slithered around. The canoe hit a log and capsized.

James would claim to have been knocked out by the impact and would remember nothing until he came to inside an ambulance.

He would tell this version to the court but when he was talking to Army investigators, he made no mention of a snake.

"There is conjecture as to how much James was involved or much did he know," Orange said. "The statement given to the army investigators is different from what he would state later in court. The statement given to the army was a written statement and the handwriting didn't seem to match his own."

A man named Ricky Hicks saw the overturned canoe, an ice chest, and a plastic bag in the river. He also saw Judy and James.

"I lost the other boy," Judy said as Ricky approached them on the shore. "A snake had gotten into the canoe and I tried to hold the snake down with a paddle."

"Where is he?"

"It's no use," Judy said, waving him off.

Hicks said Judy appeared to be concerned about James then asked him for a beer. He then drove Judy's car to a nearby phone and called the county rescue squad.

The rescue team arrived and began looking for the missing Michael.

The canoe had not moved as there was barely a current. They would find Michael's body one-quarter of a mile upriver where the canoe had been rescued. The rescuers stated that it should not have been a problem to swim upstream, suggesting that Michael could have been saved.

Judy initially said that Michael had a life jacket on but later recanted and said that it was a ski belt.

There was no ski belt on Michael when he was found.

Judy would later state that after the canoe capsized, she saw James lying face down in the water. She swam over and cleared his air passage to resuscitate him. She looked around for Michael then was picked up by Ricky Hicks.

"Michael disappeared under water," Judy said. "I went to rescue James. I almost lost both of my sons that day. Mothers just don't murder their children. If I'd have lost both of them, I don't know what I would have done. They would have had to put me in a mental institution."

"Kimberly's boyfriend would later testify that Judy had killed Michael for the insurance money," Orange said. "The children knew about their mother but she had clearly brainwashed them into silence. She provided for them, she fed them. She knew what was best."

Telling the police that she was a "clinical physician", they bought her story of the boat capsizing. The army investigators did not buy her account. Not having any evidence, however, they would eventually pay her Michael's military life insurance ($20,000). Investigators got suspicious, however, when they found out that two civilian life policies were taken out on Michael. The applications on both policies look to have been forged.

Judy's former sister-in-law, Peggy Goeller, would call to inquire how she was doing. She would make no mention of Michael's death during her first call but on a second call she told Peggy that Michael had died "during Army maneuvers".

MOVING ON

Judy would demonstrate very little grief over Michael's death and she would not be charged with his murder. Foremost on her mind was finding another man and another big check.

She opened a beauty salon in Gulf Breeze and found her next mark: businessman John Gentry.

Gentry was more well-heeled than her previous conquests so Judy put on airs for his sake. She told him that she had Ph.D.'s in biochemistry and psychology and was the former head of nursing at West Florida Hospital.

Gentry believed her story and decided to spoil his blue-blooded girlfriend expensive gifts, vacations and the finest cuisine all in the name of courtship.

Pushing the envelope, Judy would encourage John to provide life insurance for both them both. She then secretly boosted Gentry's coverage from $50,000 to $500,000 without him knowing.

Two months later, Judy began giving Gentry "vitamin pills".

"Come on," she said, placing two pills into Gentry's palm.

"What are you, my mother?" Gentry asked.

"Well, God forbid I want to see you healthy," Judy slid the cup of water toward her prey.

Gentry would then complain of dizziness and later begin vomiting after his daily dose of Judy's "vitamins."

He would admit himself into the hospital and noticed that his symptoms disappeared when he stopped taking the vitamins.

Still smitten by Judy, he did not suspect her of wrongdoing. Instead, he took her vitamins and hid them in his briefcase.

One night, however, Judy sat him down for a special dinner. She had a very special announcement.

"I'm pregnant," she said, smiling in triumph.

"Finally," Gentry said. He told Judy that they should celebrate. She told him to go to the liquor store for an expensive bottle of champagne.

"Be right back," he said, kissing her with excitement.

Running out the door, Gentry got into his car and a bomb exploded with he turned the ignition key.

Amazingly, Gentry survived the blast as trauma surgeons saved his life.

"Judy really overplayed her hand with the explosion in the car," Orange said. "Really it speaks to her level of dedication and ingenuity. Who knows where she got the idea, maybe watching the Godfather. But the police found the dynamite residue inside Gentry's car. They decided to look no further than to Judy herself."

Their interrogation and research would unearth lie after lie. They found out about the $450,000 increase in Gentry's life insurance.

Gentry himself thought the insurance had been canceled. He was shocked to learn that she had increased the payout and was paying his premiums out of her own pocket. The police didn't spare him any quarter. They would him that she was not a real doctor and that she couldn't get pregnant.

"What?" Gentry muttered, completely flabbergasted.

Judy had been sterilized seven years earlier.

Gentry couldn't believe his ears. Police would go on to say that she had booked tickets for a world cruise for herself and her children...leaving Gentry out. They discovered that Judy had been telling her friends that Gentry was suffering from a "terminal illness."

The only "terminal illness" Gentry had was Judy Buenoano.

Now fully convinced, Gentry would reach into his briefcase and give police the "vitamin pills" that Judy had been giving him.

"Judy was emptying the vitamin casing and filling it with formaldehyde and a little arsenic," Orange said. "Over time, this would have been lethal."

The state attorney would refuse to charge Judy as they wanted an air tight case in order to prosecute. Knowing that they had their killer, officers, and federal agents searched Judy's home in Gulf Breeze, obtaining wire and tape from her bedroom that looked to match the same wire/tape they found on the bomb in Gentry's car.

They would search her son James' room, finding marijuana and a sawed-off shotgun. He would be jailed him for possession of drugs and an illegal weapon.

"Again, this is a strange mistake on Judy's part," Orange said. "She was meticulous and a good liar. Why she didn't remove any and all evidence from her home is a head-scratcher. She had gotten sloppy because she had gotten away with so many crimes before without so much as a slap on the wrist. She thought she was above the law, got careless and left incriminating evidence behind."

Judy would then be arrested at her beauty salon and charged with attempted murder. It took a month of police work, but authorities would trace the source of the dynamite used in the bomb, linking the Alabama buyer to Judy via phone records which showed numerous long-distance calls from her home.

Judy would pay bail but authorities would not let up. Five months later, she would be indicted for first-degree murder in the death of her son Michael, with an additional count of grand theft for the insurance scam.

Feeling the noose around her neck, Judy would fake a seizure and wind up in Santa Rosa Hospital.

Authorities then exhumed the bodies of the men they believed she killed. Bobby Joe Morris was exhumed with arsenic found in his remains. Identical results were obtained with the exhumation of James Goodyear, in the following month.

Connecting the dots, police obtained a court order to exhume the bodies of all the men that had died while associated with Judy; son Michael, husband James Goodyear, and boyfriend Bobby Joe Morris.

Arsenic would be found in all of the bodies.

"There was enough arsenic in him (Goodyear) to kill twelve people," Detective Ted Chamberlain said. "So he was loaded. I mean that boy was loaded with it when he went down."

OPEN AND SHUT CASE

In 1984, Judy would be convicted of the murders of Michael and attempted murder of Gentry. In a separate trial in 1985, she would be convicted of the murder of James Goodyear in which she would ultimately receive the death sentence.

Judy would be imprisoned in the Florida Department of Corrections Broward Correctional Institution death row for women.

HER FINAL HOURS

Judy would spend her last day watching a hunting and fishing show, eating chocolates, and talking about old times with her children and cousin Jeanne Eaton. She would read a suspense novel called "Remember Me" and her last meal with be steamed broccoli, asparagus, strawberries and hot tea.

Judy's impending execution did not receive the same media attention as Karla Faye Tucker whose was executed only a month earlier. Her execution was opposed by the Pope and Jesse Jackson.

'"She may not have been as photogenic, as young or as pretty as Karla, but she was just as good a Christian," Eaton said.

"Judy obviously had her enablers within her family," Orange said. "How could she be 'just as good a Christian' if she is poisoning people, blowing them up and the 'Christian' she is being compared to is ice-picking people to death. People say the strangest things."

But Judy herself was bitter that no one paid much attention to her presence on death row, particularly the fact that she was a woman.

``Karla was a young female, very attractive and she had become a Christian in prison," Judy said. ``We all prayed that she would be granted a stay of execution and clemency because we felt that she was a different person and she deserved a chance. Possibly, I am a different person. But I was a Christian when I came here. I was a devout Catholic. I've not changed in that."

"It was a bit of a curiosity as to why the media was so charged to prevent the execution of Karla Faye Tucker and paid little heed to Buenoano," Orange said. "Tucker's killings were ferocious and sadistic while Buenoano's killings could be seen as passive. But what drew people to Tucker was her physical appearance and demeanor. She came across as a sweet, reformed choir girl at the end. She had a charming smile and a soft voice. Buenoano, on the other hand, looked sinister. She had squinty eyes, high cheekbones and a snarling, Southern drawl. Her body language and demeanor screamed hostile."

Judy would enter the death chamber with several guards by her side. They strapped her into the large oak chair, placing leather straps over her waist, wrists, chest, and legs.

They fitted the calf and headpiece electrodes last, inserting a wet sponge in between to reduce the burning of Judy's skin.

"Do you have a final statement?" the warden asked.

"No, sir," Judy closed her eyes tight.

The witnesses on the other side of the glass partition watched in silence.

Judy did not look at them as a leather mask was placed over her face.

The warden nodded his head and the switch was pulled.

Steam wafted up from her right leg as her body jolted for thirty-eight seconds. Her hands balled into fists, white knuckling from the shock as smoke rose from her feet to the ceiling.

Then Judy went limp. She would be pronounced dead at 7:08 a.m., March 30th, 1998.

The date was her son Michael's 37th birthday.

BLACK WIDOW KRISTIN ROSSUM

AIMEE BAXTER

Photos of a beautiful, lively little girl, her blonde hair in pigtails as she dances The Nutcracker in her little pink tutu. That same adorable child laughingly enjoying holidays with her family at their home. These are the pictures that Constance Rossum will show you of her daughter Kristin.

Bright, vivacious, and uncommonly beautiful are the words used to describe Kristin Rossum as a child. The child that everyone said was so smart and pretty, the one who modeled for department stores and who excelled in her schoolwork, the one with what seemed to be the perfect suburban childhood.

However, as many already know ... looks can be deceiving.

Idyllic Child becomes a Rebellious Teen

Born to Ralph and Constance Rossum on October 25, 1976, in Claremont, California, Kristin Rossum wanted for nothing. Kristin was the first child of Ralph Rossum – a professor at Claremont McKenna College – and his wife Constance – who worked at Azusa Pacific University. Even when her first and then second little brother was born, Kristin remained her parent's sweet little princess.

When Ralph accepted a position as President of Hampden-Sydney College in southern Virginia, the family moved across the country from California to Virginia. It was 1991 and Kristin was a delicate 15 years old. Her parents enrolled her in an all-girl boarding school in Richmond, Virginia named St. Catherine's School.

That seems to be the beginning of the end of Kristin's innocence. At the private school, Kristin made friends quickly and soon was very popular. She became the party girl smoking, drinking, and using marijuana liberally.

In 1992, at just 16 years old, Kristin is introduced to methamphetamines – a strong Central Nervous System (CNS) stimulant – and is soon hooked. Within a few weeks, she was using Crystal Meth (also known as Crank, Speed, Chalk, etc.) daily. She was a tweaker (slang used to describe a methamphetamine addict).

Kristin the Druggie

When asked about it later, Kristin recalled her first time using meth by saying "I remember it feeling good, a kind of euphoria. You feel very revved up and energetic and happy. I wanted to feel that all the time."

Soon, Kristin's straight As were slipping to become Cs and Ds. She lost weight rapidly and began to withdraw from her family and any friends who were not using meth. According to later court records, Kristin is described as having "an almost insatiable need for crystal meth."

It was not long before Kristin developed all the character traits that addicts hone to conceal and continue their freedom to use. Lying, manipulation, and theft became the new norm for young Kristin Rossum. Her parents were understandably at a loss for how to deal with this behavior. After all, not that long ago they were tucking her into her pink canopy bed and kissing her goodnight with a song and a prayer. However, the lack of consequences established by her parents could be a contributing factor in her later misdeeds.

At first, they ignored their daughter's erratic and rapidly devolving character, chalking it up to teenage angst. Eventually, they could not turn a blind eye anymore and they soon realized that their daughter was not who they thought she was.

Later, both Ralph and Constance cite an incident in 1993 as the first time they admitted their daughter had a problem. After returning from a cruise in April of that year, the Rossums found that their sweet, perfect daughter had in fact stolen their credit cards, personal checks, and a video camera.

Confronted with the missing items, Kristin pointed to some of her friends (fellow druggies) as the thieves. They say that she admitted to using some of the cash to buy drugs but insisted that the rest was stolen by somebody else. Her parents accepted Kristin's excuse and did not report the theft to police.

According to Constance's testimony later, Kristin's erratic behavior came to a head in December of 1993. Ralph Rossum – convinced Kristin was still using drugs – attempted to search his daughter's backpack. She resisted, they struggled, and he struck her several times in the arm to get the bag away from her.

However, that was not the end of the incident. Sobbing and enraged, Kristin grabbed a knife from the kitchen and slashed at her wrists. When that did not work, she ran upstairs to the bathroom, locked herself inside, and began hacking at her wrists with a razor. Later Kristin told the court, "I felt devastated ... I didn't know how to deal with the situation ... I wanted them to see how sorry I was."

Her wounds, however, were superficial and her parents treated them at home. They later said that they were "afraid of what would happen if they took her to the hospital." They feared that if they told the hospital that she had cut herself, they would have committed her for a psychiatric evaluation and if they tested her blood and found drugs, they would report her to the police.

It is likely that the reason none of the cuts were serious was that Kristin did not intend them to be. Psychologists later speculated that it was merely a way for her to manipulate her parents. If it was, it worked.

Again, Kristin escaped any immediate consequences for her bad behavior. Again, her parents made excuses for her behavior and thus enable her to continue that behavior. Cryptically, one entry in her diary after this incident contained the morbidly, prophetic words, "I could get away with murder."

A few days after this incident, a teacher noticed the marks on Kristin (or she possibly showed them to her intentionally). She called the police to the school to investigate the possibility of child abuse.

Officer Larry Horowitz of the Claremont Police investigated and testified that Kristin told him that her father had hit her and that her mother had "called her a slut and said she was worthless." After interviewing Ralph and Constance Rossum, Officer Horowitz concluded that there had been no abuse and the case was closed.

In January 1994, Constance found a glass pipe hidden in Kristin's underwear drawer. She eventually called Officer Horowitz and Kristin was handcuffed, arrested, and held for several hours at Claremont Municipal Jail.

Kristin finally had her first taste of culpability. She seemed to clean her act up and after graduating, she enrolled part-time at the University of Redlands in California. However, soon she relapsed and dropped out of school without a word to her family and simply disappeared. She moved to Chula Vista – a suburb of San Diego near the Mexican border.

A Chance Encounter

After a month of hard partying, drinking, smoking meth, and hiding from her parents, Kristin was walking the pedestrian bridge that led from Chula Vista to Tijuana, Mexico. Authorities speculate that at the time she was likely on her way to meet her supplier in Mexico on that fateful day.

As she crossed the bridge, Kristin Rossum dropped her jacket. Before she could retrieve it, a handsome young man that she later described as reminding her of John Stamos, had picked it up and was handing it to her. It was Greg de Villers and he later told friends "it was love at first sight." They chatted in French while Greg's younger brother paced nearby.

She returned to the Southern California apartment where de Villers lived with his brothers, Bertrand and Jerome, and a friend, Christopher Wren. She never left.

Within a few weeks, the couple was professing their love and de Villers had sworn to help Kristin kick her meth addiction. Greg's brothers and Wren were not happy and prompted him to end the relationship. They had noticed that things were coming up missing from the apartment since Kristin's arrival and knew of her drug problem.

According to a statement given later by de Villers' friend and roommate Christopher Wren, Kristin had told him that she felt like being with Greg was the wrong choice. For some reason, Wren chose not to tell his buddy.

Even if Wren had told de Villers about Kristin's doubts, it is unlikely that it would have made any difference. Greg de Villers was adamant, he loved Kristin Rossum no matter what her faults and he was going to save her from herself.

By May of 1995, it looked as though he had done just that. By all accounts, it looked like Kristin was clean and free of the hold meth had on her. She reestablished contact with her worried parents and it looked like Kristin was finally moving towards the bright future her parents had envisioned for their little girl.

The Rossums looked at Greg de Villers as if he was an angel for all that he had done for Kristin. Constance Rossum, in an interview with the CBS news magazine "48 Hours," put it like this, "We always called Greg our godsend from heaven. I mean, of all the people she could have met, to have met a nice, decent person who wanted to take care of her, we thanked God."

Soon, Kristin enrolled at San Diego State University. Her professors later said described Rossum as a stellar student with one going so far as to describe her as "among the most promising students" he had "ever taught."

Everyone who knew her believed she was happy. She was earning straight As and in 1998, she graduated cum laude (with honors). She got a job at San Diego Medical Examiner's office as a toxicologist.

Constance would later testify, "Our old Kristin was back," and she thanked God and de Villers – in that order – for the change.

Storybook Love?

Everyone who knew them described Kristin and Greg as the perfect couple. Constance Rossum testified later that when they were together they were "like a couple of lovebirds." When they announced their engagement, nobody was surprised.

However, as is often the case, outward appearances did not accurately represent reality. There was a layer of tension beneath the surface of de Villers and Rossum's storybook love affair. Kristin's closest friends knew that she had a hard time staying faithful and monogamous.

According to prosecutor's later, Kristin actually maintained a "graphically flirtatious" correspondence with a former boyfriend and at least one other man during at least some portion of her relationship with de Villers. Rossum even went to her mother only a month before she was supposed to walk down the aisle and broke down in tears as she told her mother that she wanted to cancel the wedding.

Constance Rossum considered her daughter's outburst to be cold feet, pre-wedding jitters that would pass. After all, Greg de Villers was the man who led her out of the darkness of addiction and Constance could not see how Kristin could possibly want to end the relationship.

She would soon tell the court, "I gave her the wrong counsel, I'm afraid."

The wedding was spectacular. The video shows a smiling and laughing Kristin Rossum, now Kristin de Villers, dancing with her new husband and looking happy. As for de Villers, he is recorded on that video saying, "Kristin is the most wonderful person I've ever met. I just can't wait to spend the rest of my life with her."

Only seven months after the wedding, however, Kristin Rossum told her mother that she felt "trapped like a bird in a cage." It was January 2000 and Kristin's journal shows that she had begun souring on her marriage only a couple of months after the wedding.

Greg de Villers did not show any sign that he felt the same or even knew of his wife's misgivings and doubt. Conversely, his brother Jerome later testified that Greg was ecstatically happy and never spoke of anything even smacking of marital discord. Even his colleagues at a genetics research firm where de Villers worked, described him as happily married and devoted to his wife. Some even went so far as to describe Greg de Villers as "sickeningly in love with his wife."

Friends of Greg de Villers said that he was often talking about his plans for their future together. He bragged about his wife's accomplishments, both big and small, and often spoke of starting a family. One friend remembers him saying that he wanted "all girls who were as beautiful and smart as Kristin."

At the same time, his adored wife was painting a much grimmer portrait of her marriage and her husband. She often complained to colleagues and friends about Greg, saying that he was moody, controlling, and domineering. Later, in an interview with "48 Hours," Kristin said, "Greg became very, very clinging... I tried to pull away and have some sort of independence."

An email sent to her brother Brent only 11 months after the wedding showed how she truly felt. She wrote, "I should have trusted my own instincts and called off the wedding. Now I'm stuck with the heavy realization that I married the wrong person."

A New Love Affair

Not long after Kristin Rossum sent that email to her brother, she met Dr. Michael Robertson. Newly hired as Chief Toxicologist at the San Diego Medical Examiner's office, Robertson was Kristin's immediate supervisor and she began spending large amounts of time with him.

Soon, they were spending time together outside of work. Kristin found danger and excitement in her passionate affair with her handsome, Australian doctor – who was also married. Her husband – and the problems she seemed to have with him – disappeared from Kristin's consideration and soon she was talking with friends outside of her colleagues about the wonderful new man in her life who she described as "a big hunk of an Australian guy."

By early May, Rossum was receiving inappropriate emails and notes from her boss. A search of her desk later turned up love notes and IOUs for things such as "a night of lovemaking" from Robertson. Coworkers later reported that Robertson was often seen sauntering into work with a bouquet of flowers that would soon end up on Rossum's desk.

In June, according to court records, Kristin Rossum had given her lover a gift. A book titled "52 Invitations To Great Sex" she had inscribed on the inside cover, "Well, sweetheart, together we'll enjoy a lifetime of passion."

When asked later, Rossum said, "I felt like I was in love. It was very romantic, very exciting, very passionate."

In August of 2000, Kristin turned to her best friend, Melissa Prager. Prager later told the court that he friend confided in her that she was madly in love with Robertson but was "terrified" by the idea of telling Greg she wanted a divorce.

In October 2000, Greg de Villers was still telling his friends, family, co-workers, and anyone else who would listen about his love for his wife and his plans for their future. His brother Jerome later told the court that around Halloween, Greg was talking about his excitement over taking his future children with Kristin out to trick or treat.

However, Kristin Rossum had reached a conclusion about her marriage. She told her close friends that she was looking for an apartment and planned to leave her husband.

'Til Death Do Us Part

It is unclear how de Villers learned of his wife's infidelity and plan to leave him. Rossum has always claimed that she told Greg de Villers about the affair and that her admission launched a spiraling depression in her husband.

According to Kristin Rossum, she told her husband about Robertson and he demanded the man's phone number. When Kristin supplied the number (although why she would is uncertain), de Villers called her boss and lover and demanded that he break off their relationship.

There is no court record of a response to this demand by Robertson. However, the relationship continued.

Authorities, however, have a very different set of circumstances in mind for how Greg discovered Kristin's infidelity.

They maintain that de Villers found out about the affair on accident in the fall of 2000. This was after Kristin and Robertson were sent to Milwaukee together to attend a toxicology conference. According to court records, despite being booked into separate hotels – likely due to rumors in the office about their relationship – the duo rented their own room together and spent several nights from September 30 to October 7 together in that room.

A coworker saw Kristin at the conference during the week and noted that she was no longer wearing her wedding ring.

One of the conferences that Rossum and Robertson attended in Milwaukee was on the deadly effects of fentanyl. Fentanyl is a clear, odorless narcotic that is 100 times stronger than morphine. It is generally administered to cancer patients whose pain is not eased by other means. It is so potent that it only takes a few drops to kill.

The seminar also discussed the fact that the drug is so rarely prescribed and used that most medical examiner's offices do not test for it. Both Rossum and Robertson were well aware of the fact that their office did not test for fentanyl.

During the three years that Rossum had worked in the San Diego Medical Examiner's office, only seven cases of death by overdose had involved fentanyl. She had seen 15 patches and 1 vial of the drug in a powder form. It was Rossum's job to log and track the drugs in her logbook. It was Robertson's job to hold the key to the cabinet those substances was then stored in.

These were facts that seemed innocuous at the time but would soon hold a more serious meaning.

Returning to Old Ways

Only a day or two after returning from Milwaukee, Rossum sent de Villers an email telling him that she was taking three different prescription drugs "to help with the severe anxiety I've been experiencing as a result of our relationship. You've hurt me beyond repair."

Not only was Kristin taking prescription medications, she had fallen back into her addiction to meth. After some of the drugs went missing from her office, Robertson admitted later that he found traces of the drug in her desk and rather than turning his girlfriend in, he flushed the drugs down the toilet. Then he covered for her with his superiors.

Once again, Kristin Rossum has done something bad. Once again, somebody shields her from the ramifications of her actions. Once again, there are no consequences for Kristin's bad actions.

Severing Ties

By early November 2000, Rossum was ready to end her relationship with de Villers. She insisted she wanted only a "trial separation."

She later told detectives that de Villers literally collapsed when she told him she was leaving him. She claimed that he lay in bed for days afterward and would not communicate with her. She later told the court, "It was painful for me, too, to see someone you love hurt so much." She still never owned up to the fact that it was her own actions that caused her husband that pain.

On November 6, 2000, just after 9:15 pm, Kristin Rossum called 991.

She claimed that her husband was unresponsive and that she was doing CPR to try and revive him. When paramedics arrived, however, they found Rossum on the phone in the living room. Her husband was lying lifeless on their bed.

Gregory de Villers lay dead in his La Jolla bedroom with rose petals covering his chest. Besides his lifeless head lay a copy of his wedding picture ... less than two years old. Nearby on the floor lay a crumpled love letter from the dashing Australian doctor that was his wife's boss and lover. Beside that was his wife's discarded diary, open to an entry that she had left confiding that she felt her marriage was the biggest mistake of her life.

For all intents and purposes, it looked like a suicide. His distraught widow claimed that Greg had learned that her affair with Robertson was still happening.

However, de Villers' brother Jerome adamantly refused to accept that his brother had committed suicide. The entire de Villers family demanded an investigation. Still, the San Diego police were hesitant to open an investigation.

The Truth and Nothing but the Truth

Their opinion quickly changed and authorities soon came to suspect Kristin Rossum, de Villers' 26-year-old blonde beauty of a wife. They believed that she had used her knowledge as a toxicologist and the information that she had gleaned from working in the medical examiner's office to poison her husband.

Due to concerns over a conflict of interest, de Villers' autopsy was outsourced to another lab in Los Angeles. That lab is one of the few in the country that tests for fentanyl. They found 7 times the lethal dose of fentanyl in de Villers' system.

Two weeks after de Villers' death, the San Diego police brought Kristin Rossum in for interrogation. She reiterated to police that her husband had been extremely depressed.

According to Kristin Rossum's story, on the Thursday before de Villers' death, they struggled over a letter that she had sticking out of her back pocket. In her account, de Villers' attempted to grab the letter from her pocket and knocked her to the ground to wrest it from her. She claimed that it was the first time she had been afraid of her husband.

When he had the letter, as Rossum's story goes, he held it out and threatened to take it to his wife's office and expose the affair as well as her reoccurring meth addiction. She took the letter and shredded it but de Villers pieced it back together.

In court, Rossum's parents described the night, two days before de Villers' death, when they went over to visit the couple for dinner. Ralph Rossum testified that de Villers seemed to be deeply depressed, "a man spiraling down."

Kristin Rossum's father continued to describe how de Villers had drunk heavily that night. He drank wine and gin until his father in law had to tell him to lower his voice. Constance Rossum described

Greg de Villers' voice as "fraught with melodrama" as he spoke at length about the dozen red roses that he had given to Kristin for her birthday a few days earlier.

She testified that he seemed depressed, agitated, and particularly obsessed with the fact that all but one had died and shed its petals. In a TV interview, she gave months after the death, Rossum stated, "He was making a big deal of the last rose standing. I think he was just making a statement that he knew our relationship was over."

Things rapidly spiraled from that point on. Police learned that Rossum had relapsed and was using meth again.

On June 25, 2001 – 7 months after Greg de Villers' death – his wife was arrested on charges of First Degree Murder. She spent over six months in jail and then on January 4, 2002, her parents posted $1.25 million for bail.

During the trial, the prosecution contended that she killed her husband to keep him from telling her bosses that she was having an affair with Robertson and that she was stealing meth from the office. They presented evidence that she had the knowledge about fentanyl to use it, access to the drug (remember the missing fentanyl from her office), and the motive to kill her husband.

On November 12, 2002, Kristin Rossum was found guilty of first-degree murder.

Exactly one month later on December 12, she was sentenced to life in prison without the chance of parole. She was transferred from the San Diego jail to the Central California Women's Facility in Chowchilla California – the largest women's correctional facility in the United States.

Distant Repercussions

In 2006, the de Villers family filed a lawsuit against Rossum and San Diego County for wrongful death. They were asking for $50 million but on March 25, 2006, a San Diego jury ordered Rossum to pay more than $100 million in punitive damages to the de Villers family. The same judge ordered San Diego County to pay $1.5 million.

According to the de Villers' lawyer John Gomez, the punitive damages awarded in this case are the most assessed against an individual defendant in California history. The jury apparently awarded double what the de Villers' family was asking for due to the estimation that Rossum could make $60 million from selling the rights to her story.

The judge later lowered the awarded amounts to $10 million in punitive damages and $4.5 million in a compensatory award.

In September of 2010, a 3-judge panel of the 9th US Circuit Court of Appeals ruled that Rossum's lawyers should have challenged the prosecutions assertion that she poisoned her husband with fentanyl by demanding their own tests. Due to this, the panel ordered a San Diego federal court to hold a hearing into whether the defense's error could have affected the trial's outcome.

On September 13, 2011, the US Court of Appeals withdrew its opinion and replaced it with a one-paragraph statement that denied Rossum's petition.

Conclusion

Kristin Rossum will spend the rest of her life behind bars. She has exhausted her state appeals and the federal courts denied her petition to be heard.

Her contention remains that her husband killed himself. She further believes that he did it the way that he did to point the finger of guilt at her. She vehemently insists that she did not kill her husband.

At one point, Kristin Rossum even suggested that her lover the handsome Australian doctor might have killed her husband. He knew about de Villers' threat to expose them before his death and had access to the fentanyl.

For his part, Robertson returned to Brisbane, Australia only one month after de Villers' death under the excuse that he had to care for his ailing mother. In September of 2013, the San Diego Reader reported that prosecutors filed a criminal complaint against Robertson in 2006 charging him with one count of conspiracy to obstruct justice.

If he returned to the US, Robertson could face up to three years in prison. In 2001, Robertson was named as an "unindicted co-conspirator" in Rossum's trial.

As of 2014, Robertson was running a forensic consulting business in Brisbane.

Kristin Rossum, the sweet spoiled only daughter of college professors, who was never held accountable for her actions as she grew up will spend the rest of her days within the walls of the largest women's correctional facility in the US. She is finally going to have to answer for what she has done.

BLACK WIDOW LYDA TRUEBLOOD

JESSI DILLARD

A true "black widow"

Death followed Lyda Trueblood everywhere she went. At first glance, it may have seemed that the young woman was facing a run of bad luck – but as the run continued, suspicions began to arise.

Northeast of Kansas City, in the small town of Keytesville, Missouri, a true "black widow" was born on October 16, 1892. Over the course of her life, Lyda Anna Mae Trueblood took on seven married names, and is most well-known as Lyda Southard. However, Idaho remembers her as Lady Bluebeard – the state's first female serial killer.

"She swept the men of her choice off their feet – courted them so persistently that they could not escape," said V. H. Ormsby, a deputy sheriff from Twin Falls, Idaho. Ormsby was one of the officers who arrested Trueblood in Honolulu for the death of her fourth husband.

By the age of 27, Trueblood had already killed six people, including her own daughter. However, she would only be convicted of one murder – the poisoning of her fourth husband, Edward Meyer, in 1921.

"The marital experiences of the one-time Missouri country town girl eclipses even those of fiction. Ten years ago, while still in her teens, she was attending Sunday school and enjoying the popularity that goes with being a village belle."

Described as "pudgy faced and plain of figure," Trueblood still caught the eye of Robert Dooley, whose family was close with Trueblood's. Some said Trueblood was the most popular girl at her high school, claiming she had an "indefinable something, a spark giving off a light that draws men, by physiological and chemical attraction."

"They wasn't so wealthy, just so-so," said Mrs. Larrabee Hanson, who lived near the Trueblood family. "But they were all church-going people, devout and clean-living. (Trueblood) went to church every Sunday without fail."

A magazine writer, Alan Jaffe, who detailed Trueblood's history for a profile in *Argosy* magazine in 1957, said men "hung around her like flies about a honey pot." In fact, when Trueblood finally left her childhood home and moved to Twin Falls, Robert Dooley followed – and the two were married there in 1912, when she was only 21.

A promise of the future

"They had a perfectly normal relationship," said Mychel Matthews with the Twin Falls County Historical Museum. "They appeared to be just like the rest of the residents around town."

With the security of their future family in mind, the newlyweds decided to take out an insurance policy on Robert and his brother, Edward. If either died, the survivor would inherit $1,000 – with an equal amount going to Trueblood. And by August 1915, the couple was $2,000 richer. Edward Dooley had fallen ill and had died after just a few days – typhoid, the doctors said.

"There was nothing suspicious about the death," Matthews said. "It was ruled as food poisoning or typhoid."

As Edward lay dying, Trueblood convinced her husband to revise his insurance policy – for the family's protection, she argued. A new policy was drafted for Robert and his wife, stating that if either died, the surviving spouse would receive $2,000.

Just one month later, Robert Dooley followed in his brother's footsteps – succumbing to typhoid in a similar fashion. Trueblood, however, had begun to build herself a substantial nest egg. Only six weeks after losing her husband, Trueblood's infant daughter, Laura Marie, "drank from a contaminated well," according to reports – leaving the widow lonely and desperate for companionship.

Since accidental poisonings did occasionally occur in rural areas, and epidemics – particularly typhoid – were rampant during that time, the deaths of the Dooleys were only briefly investigated by authorities.

"Little children died all the time, at that period of history," Matthews said. "She probably got a lot of sympathy, 'oh, that poor woman. She's lost her daughter, her husband, all to this stomach flu.'"

Trueblood endured a brief but mandatory period of mourning after losing her family, but soon struck up a relationship with a waiter at her favorite Twin Falls restaurant. William McHaffie married Trueblood just two years after the loss of her first husband and only child, and the couple immediately sought an insurance policy for William. Trueblood was named as William's only beneficiary, to receive $5,000 if anything was to happen to him.

The couple moved to Hardin, Montana, and only a year after they married, William died of "influenza." According to his friends and customers, William had always been a robust, healthy man – and the speed and depth of his sudden illness shocked them.

"Lyda Trublood was very careful," said crime author Diane Fanning. "She waited until they actually got sick – then, it was easier to believe that they had died of an illness. Everybody thought it was something he ate that finally did him in, but all that it was, really, was Lyda Trueblood."

Unfortunately for Trueblood, however, William had failed to pay the second premium on his insurance policy, letting it lapse. Trueblood received nothing for her efforts. Days after her late husband's funeral, Trueblood sold all her property and disappeared.

Moving on

After relocating to Denver, Trueblood managed to ensnare another victim – a farm machinery salesman she had met during her previous marriage to William. In fact, William had told friends that after he'd come to their door in an attempt to make a sale, Trueblood had seemed "struck" by him – and neighbours reported that the happy couple had even started fighting more after that.

Trueblood married Harlan Lewis in March of 1919, and took him with her back to Montana. The couple settled in Billings, and only one month later, Harlan took out a $10,000 life insurance policy. According to Matthews, the larger policies are an indication that

Trueblood was manipulating the men in order to receive greater payouts.

"(Trueblood) was motivated by one thing, and one thing only - greed," said former FBI profiler Candice Delong. "She wanted money."

By mid-July, just three months after the wedding, disaster had struck. After falling ill to a sudden case "ptomaine poisoning," Harlan left Trueblood a widow for the third time – and this time, the cheque came through. After cashing out the estate, Trueblood disappeared again. Instead of heading somewhere new, however, Trueblood decided to return to Idaho.

Under the name of Lyda McHaffie, Trueblood checked into the Rogerson Hotel in Twin Falls in May 1919, and found herself a job at the Grille Café on Main Avenue. Business at the café picked up immediately, reports claim, and the foreman of Ira Perrine's Blue Lake Ranch, Edward Meyer, started visiting the restaurant regularly.

"Folks couldn't help noticing that the air sort of shimmered when (Trueblood's) eyes met Ed's," wrote Jaffe in his profile. "And that the ham he got was thicker, the eggs sunnier than those served other patrons."

The very next month, Trueblood moved to Pocatello, Idaho, where she married Edward Meyer and settled on a ranch.

"She rigged herself out fit to kill, bought a long mink coat and a closed car. Everybody in town was talking about the way she ran around to dances," said Ormsby. "She talked around town that she wasn't in love with Ed, but she wanted a home, and she said that sometime she might learn to love him."

Although she had started going by the name "Anna McHaffie," Trueblood showed no other signs of leaving her past life behind her. She applied for an insurance policy in Edward's name the day after the wedding, in the amount of $10,000 – however, the policy was not approved, and reasons were never clarified. It's possible that insurance companies were beginning to wise up to the run of bad luck Trueblood had encountered.

Suspicious situation

Only two weeks after the couple had wed, on August 25, Edward took ill. Doctors at the hospital claimed he had an excellent chance of recovery, but he was dead by September 7.

"She didn't wait for him to get sick," said Matthews. "Maybe she grew impatient, and that was probably the mistake she made in all of this."

Trueblood's previous husbands had been fairly low-key, unlikely to attract attention despite the unbelievable series of coincidences that had resulted in their deaths – and Trueblood's subsequent insurance claims. Edward Meyer, however, was a different case. As a prominent figure in Twin Falls, Edward had dealings with many of the leading business and farm people in the region – including the Twin Falls county sheriff.

"The townsfolk weren't just satisfied," Ormsby said. "They started a lot of talk, and the insurance company held up payment on the policy. The matter got into politics and folks wanted to know what the candidates for sheriff would do about (Trueblood)."

When traces of arsenic were discovered during a routine post-mortem examination, detectives finally brought the widow in for questioning.

"The investigation was just getting underway when the woman disappeared," stated an article published in the New York Times on May 13, 1921. "Detectives traced her to Los Angeles, and kept track of her while the bodies of the two (Dooleys), the infant daughter, and McHaffie were exhumed and portions of the viscera were sent to chemists."

Edward Meyer's death had become somewhat of a political issue in the 1920 campaign for sheriff, and potential candidates were asked how they planned to handle the case. The current sheriff passed the case to a "remarkable" deputy, Virgin Ormsby – and the investigation would be virtually his only assignment for months.

"After she left for California, the town got more dissatisfied than ever, and in January, I was assigned to the case," Ormsby said. "I've had the bodies of the men dissatisfied and examined – three chemists each working separately reported to me that they found arsenic. I interviewed the doctors who attended the husbands and obtained statements from them that enabled me to build a strong case against her."

Ormsby even discovered that a relative of Trueblood's first husband and brother-in-law had been studying the suspicious deaths in his family. A chemist named Earl Dooley had already begun to consider the possibility that Robert and Edward Dooley had been poisoned with arsenic – and according to Fanning, his suspicions led him to investigate the scene of Trueblood's most recent victim.

After taking samples from Edward Meyer's vomit in the sand, Earl had them tested.

"Sure enough, he found arsenic – and when that happened, he went to a doctor to get it confirmed in another lab," Fanning said. "It was definitely arsenic."

Mounting evidence

Police first determined that the Dooley brothers had been poisoned, as well as Trueblood's own child. Officers in Montana started investigating the cases of Harlan Lewis and William McHaffie, intrigued by the seemingly impossible coincidences that had led Trueblood to make so many insurance claims. Trueblood, meanwhile, was busy seducing her fifth husband, Paul Southard, in Los Angeles – while prosecutor Frank L. Stephen started building a case against her back in Twin Falls.

While working odd jobs, saving her money, and reportedly describing herself as a nurse, Trueblood managed to convince Paul to propose. The two were married in November of 1920. Although Paul, who served as a seaman in the navy, claimed he needed no additional insurance coverage beyond typical provisions, Ormsby learned that a policy had in fact been taken out on Chief Petty Officer Paul Southard – with Trueblood named as the beneficiary.

Shortly after they were wed, Paul was transferred from Los Angeles to Pearl Harbour, and his new bride joined him in Hawaii. Ormsby was in hot pursuit, having tracked Trueblood with the help of California law enforcement. Officers in Honolulu received a warrant for Trueblood's arrest in May 1921. She was picked up on May 12 to return to Boise, Idaho, for her trial – with her husband Paul at her side.

"She's been a mighty good wife to me," said Paul, who refused to believe the charges, "and I don't care if she married ten men before, and they all died. That wouldn't make her a murderess."

Although tabloids had already started running headlines about the gruesome tale, labelling Trueblood catchy names like "Lethal Lyda" or "The Arsenic Widow," Trueblood maintained her innocence as she and Paul prepared to catch the *Matsonia* out of Honolulu. Some reports claimed she was acting "like any lucky vacationer about to embark on an ocean cruise," her neck heavy with flowered leis.

"I am entirely innocent, and I look forward to the trip with optimism," Trueblood said in a brief statement to the press. "I am anxious to get back to Twin Falls and face my accusers."

At the jail, Trueblood finally granted an interview to reporter Hazel Pedlar Faulkner, with the San Francisco Examiner. Pedlar Faulkner described the accused as "dainty, friendly, and refined" – not exactly the picture of a "sinister murderer," she said.

"I have been nervous because of my imprisonment and the unnecessary disgrace to my husband," Pedlar Faulkner quotes Trueblood as saying. "I know as well as anything that I can clear myself. The evidence gathered against me is purely circumstantial. Their work is to prove the charges, and that will not be easy because of the documents I hold."

Trueblood claimed that her husbands had died because she was a "typhoid carrier," and even stated that she had nothing to do with the large life insurance policies her late husbands had all secured before their untimely deaths.

"Life insurance was no object to me," stated Trueblood in Pedlar Faulkner's interview. "I have had enough money. And what insurance my husbands carried were business propositions they took out without regard to me or without consulting me, generally."

Before leaving San Francisco to bring Trueblood back to Boise, Ormsby and his wife, Nellie, took the accused for one last night on the town. After having dinner at a restaurant and strolling through a downtown shopping district, the Ormsbys and their charge attended a vaudeville show at the Orpheum Theatre.

Although Trueblood was trying to remain under the radar, a San Francisco Chronicle reporter recognized her – and wrote about her activities the next morning.

"With the grim specters of four dead husbands, a brother-in-law, and her infant baby hovering near her, while the accusing finger of the law points at her and charges murder, Mrs. Lyda Eva Southard, psychological enigma, calmly spent yesterday seeing the sights of San Francisco," read Herb Westen's article in the San Francisco Call and Post.

"She smiles, a trifle shyly perhaps, but a bored light creeps around her eyes as if to her it is all a tedious legal jumble, which will steal precious hours from her pursuit of happiness."

Up to the jury

Despite Trueblood's denial of the charges, the state contended that she'd fed Edward Meyer, her fourth husband, hefty doses of arsenic extracted from flypaper. Trueblood denied it and the state presented further evidence – largely circumstantial, but it was still enough for a conviction.

The trial, which started on October 3 and lasted six weeks, received attention nation-wide. At the time, it would become the longest criminal trial in history. Witnesses were called from Missouri, Montana, Tennessee, and California – a total of 182 named to appear, but not all were called to the stand.

Prosecutor Stephen tried desperately to bring in Buddy Thornberg to testify against Trueblood – a reporter for the Daily News in Twin Falls who had come close to marrying Trueblood shortly before she snagged Edward Meyer. He'd met the widow at the café, and she had swept him off his feet. According to reports, Thornberg had told his friends he would be marrying the "rich widow from Montana," and – on her advice – he was considering taking out an additional private insurance policy on top of the $10,000 government policy he already had in place.

After his friends managed to convince him to not follow through with a marriage, however, Thornberg had ended his relationship with Trueblood and was presumed to have moved to Washington – never to be heard from again.

An article claimed that "every session of the trial found the court auditorium filled to capacity, principally by women and girls." Another report claimed the trail was, "draggy," and "rather technical – arsenic versus typhoid, laboratory tests versus the official death certificate. This certificate, giving typhoid as the cause of death, was more or less (Trueblood's) sole defense."

The whole case presented against Trueblood suggested that she didn't particularly love her husband, and could have – and likely did – poison him. Not only that, she took out insurance on his life, and fled immediately after his death.

According to Ormsby, a visit to the McHaffies' home in Montana had uncovered evidence to back up this theory. He'd discovered a "large quantity" of cut-up flypaper containing arsenic in the basement, with residue of arsenic in a pot Trueblood had likely used to boil the poison out – before serving it to her husband in tainted food.

"(Trueblood) went about her killing very deliberately," Fanning said. "She bought out everything the store had in flypaper. It was obvious that she wanted to have a permanent supply on hand."

An article published in the New York Times on October 9, 1921 stated that under the questioning of Prosecuting Attorney Frank Stephen, Dr E. F. Roberbaugh, state chemist, confirmed the presence of arsenic poison in the body of Edward Meyer when he examined the body in April of that year.

"The witness testified he found .05 milligrams of poison in five grams of a specimen of several internal organs and .10 milligrams in a ten-gram quantity of the specimen," the article read. "The witness said the distribution of poison throughout the system was not equal and he estimated that a little less than five grains of poison probably was contained in Meyer's body."

He added that the findings "virtually duplicated" those obtained immediately after Edward Meyer's death in September, 1920.

The state requested permission to introduce further evidence relating to the deaths of Trueblood's other husbands, and the judge ruled the testimony admissible. While physicians did, in some instances, contradict testimony of other expert witnesses on the question of cause of death, analysis made by three separate chemists agreed that poison was present in all bodies exhumed.

"She poisoned their food, and over time, the arsenic would build up," said Fanning. "Most of the death certificates all said some sort of stomach ailment."

After a deliberation of twenty-three hours, the jury came back with a verdict on November 4, 1921. Trueblood was found guilty of second-degree murder. Speculation was that the jury had "blanched" at the thought of hanging a woman, but there was no doubt that she had done it. Even her husband, Paul Southard, filed for divorce after watching the trial.

"Lyda Trueblood was a classic black widow," Delong said. "And she did it for money."

According to an article in the November 5, 1921 issue of the Sacramento Union, Trueblood showed "no sign of feeling," and didn't even raise her eyes from the floor as the verdict was read. This was typical of Trueblood's attitude throughout the trial, however.

"On the stand, the accused woman maintained an unperturbed attitude throughout a long grilling by the prosecution, which failed to adduce any important admissions from her," the article stated.

Only eight years after Trueblood's incarceration, Ormsby suffered a paralytic stroke and died in his wife's arms. His obituary ran on the front page of the December 30, 1929 edition of the Twin Falls Times – and flowers were delivered to his funeral, sent from a Lyda Southard.

A "break for freedom"

Still, the guilty verdict and the sentence of at least ten years in prison wasn't enough to keep Trueblood from seducing men.

"She proved that no prison walls can hold her, and made her escape from the Idaho State Penitentiary by fascinating, as did Milady, a prison guard, who is believed to have rigged up for her an ingenious ladder of plumbers' pipes and torn blankets and garden hose," read an article published in the October 25, 1931 issue of the Salt Lake Tribune. "This guard, however, died before (Trueblood) made her break for freedom."

According to the article, Trueblood had already served ten years of her sentence and was eligible for parole when she made her great escape on May 4, 1931. The ladder, fashioned for her by prison guard Jack Watkins, had been buried for months beneath the prison walls. Watkins had also provided Trueblood with a saw, which she used to remove a bar from her cell window.

"The escape itself was dramatic," the article continued. "Women inmates, evidently under the spell of the woman, who could fascinate those of her own sex as well as men, staged a party and played the phonograph and sang while she was gaining her way to liberty."

Trueblood ran right into the arms of David Minton. Minton, an ex-convict himself, had fallen under Trueblood's spell while he was still behind bars. After he helped Trueblood escape from prison, she'd ended the relationship. Leaving him alive was a mistake, however – enraged, Minton went to the police and told them they could find Trueblood in Topeka, Kansas.

This, however, was not before a nation-wide manhunt was organized to attempt to locate Trueblood, who was described by Warden R. E. Thomas of the Idaho State Penitentiary as "one of the most dangerous criminals at large."

"Some man will probably pay with his life in agony and death before this ruthless woman can again be brought to justice," he said. "That she is the modern 'Mrs. Bluebeard' is certain."

In fact, before the police found her in Kansas, Trueblood had managed to swindle another man into marrying her. Harry Whitlock, who later described Trueblood as a "model wife," was shocked when the police showed up looking for her. The relationship had begun when Trueblood, calling herself "Fern," had started doing housekeeping work for Whitlock – and she had suggested he take out a $20,000 life insurance policy, but it hadn't been purchased before she asked him for some travel money and took off.

Fifteen months after her escape, Trueblood was returned to Boise – with her marriage to Whitlock annulled.

Back in prison, Trueblood continued to seduce her prey. This time, she set her sights on George Rudd, a prison warden. She managed to convince him to grant her special privileges – frequent day trip to a local resort, visitation to see her sick mother, and even transportation to Boise to see movies. However, when authorities discovered that he'd been treating Trueblood to these privileges, Rudd was forced to resign from his position.

Free at last

Finally, Trueblood was paroled from prison on October 3, 1941, and fully pardoned only one year later.

"I think they figured that she had lost most of her good looks and charm, and was no longer a menace to society," Matthews said.

After spending a few years living with her sister, Blanche Quigley, in Nyssa, Oregon, Trueblood returned to her family's farm at Twin Falls – but the local townspeople and even her relatives weren't pleased to see her.

A few months later, Trueblood left for Provo, Utah, where no one knew her, and pulled together the funds to purchase a small secondhand shop. There, she married her seventh husband, Hal Shaw. However, once Shaw's children discovered who she was and learned about her unsavory past, he vanished – leaving her to move to Salt Lake City, where she worked for several years as a housekeeper and waitress.

"You wonder, did (the husbands) ever suspect that it was not a natural illness that was making them suffer in agony," Fanning said. "We can only hope that they never understood what was really happening."

Trueblood died of a heart attack on February 5, 1958 in Salt Lake City. Her body remains at Sunset Memorial Park in Twin Falls, Idaho, where she was buried as Anna E. Shaw. Still, some report seeing a ghost bearing Trueblood's likeness haunting the halls of the Idaho prison to this day – the prison's most notorious inmate, maintaining a presence even after her death.

"When she finally died, it was from a heart attack," Fanning said. "It's amazing to think that (Trueblood) actually had a heart."